MORALITY AND
THE ADOLESCENT

MORALITY AND THE ADOLESCENT

A Pastoral Psychology Approach

Charles M. Shelton

CROSSROAD • NEW YORK

1991

The Crossroad Publishing Company
370 Lexington Avenue, New York, N.Y. 10017

Printed in the United States of America

Library of Congress Cataloging-in-Publication Data

Shelton, Charles M.
    Morality and the adolescent : a pastoral psychology approach /
Charles M. Shelton.
        p.   cm.
    Bibliography: p.
    Includes index.
    ISBN 0–8245–0910–2; 0–8245–1134–4 (pbk):
        1. Church work with youth.   2. Church work with youth—Catholic
Church.   3. Youth—Pastoral counseling of.   4. Moral development.
5. Adolescent psychology.   6. Youth—Conduct of life.   7. Youth-
-Religious life.   8. Catholic Church—Clergy.   I. Title.
BV4447.S54   1989
253.5'088055—dc19

Acknowledgment is gratefully made for permission to adapt for this book articles
that appeared in the following journals: *Spirituality Today* 34, Winter 1982; *Religious
Education* 79, no. 2, by permission of the Religious Education Association; *The Living
Light* 22, no. 4 (June 1986) by permission of the Department of Education of the
United States Catholic Conference; *Occasional Papers # 6*, Center for Youth Ministry
Development, Naugatuck, Connecticut; and *The Journal of the Catholic Campus Minis-
try Association* 1, no. 2.

To Dan McGann—
my brother and friend

Contents

Contents

Acknowledgments

When writing a book one soon learns the need to acknowledge the help and support of others. There are several people I wish to thank in a special way. First, the members of the Department of Psychiatry at the Indiana University School of Medicine who were my colleagues during my clinical psychology internship year. In particular, I am indebted to James Gange, Ph.D., George Karwisch, Ph.D., and John Thompson, M.D. I owe a very special debt of gratitude to Matt Galvin, M.D. Through several stimulating conversations he helped me to clarify my own thinking in the area of conscience development. I also wish to thank the graduate clinical faculty of Loyola University of Chicago, in particular my colleagues Dan McAdams, Ph.D., and Patricia Rupert, Ph.D. The clinical and academic training I received at Loyola has taught me the true role of the clinician as both scientist and artist. I am also indebted to my brother Jesuits with whom I lived at Brebeuf Jesuit High School for providing me a supportive environment in which to write. Finally, I owe a deep debt of thanks to Mike Barber, S. J., and Matt Gamber, S. J. Their kindness, support, and sense of humor have taught me the true meaning of Jesuit brother.

Introduction

One of the most encouraging signs in interdisciplinary studies today is the dialogue taking place between psychology and theology. The former has moved from a rigid and mechanistic view of the human person to a rediscovery of values and their relation to human thinking and behavior. Psychology's new emphasis on values is particularly relevant in recent writing in developmental psychology: not only are psychologists examining behaviors and reinforcing experiences, they are giving attention to the subjective experience of personal meaning and its centrality for human growth. Current psychological theory has shown sensitivity to the purpose, goals, and intentionality that are present in human experience and that have an impact on behavior.

Correspondingly, theologians are more inclined than ever to appreciate the struggles and developmental needs that preoccupy all individuals and that take on added significance for adolescents. Moreover, theologians are discovering that for moral norms to have meaning in any life situation, they must incorporate the concrete, existential reality in which a person's moral decisions take place. This perspective embraces not only the "human" aspects of life, but the environment in which one's moral decisions are made.

This bridging of psychological and theological viewpoints is important for the study of adolescent moral development. To be sure, any discussion of this topic from a Christian perspective cherishes the Christian ideal contained in the Gospel's call to discipleship. Yet, what is certainly important and all too often absent in such approaches is a comprehensive understanding of the adolescent's experience. Stated simply, moral growth cannot be explained through rarefied theological discussion; rather, it is an ongoing life experience of everyday involvement in which human needs and ideals come together in deepening commitment.

As a priest and a student of psychology, I have had the opportunity over the past decade to minister in a variety of roles to young people in secondary school and college. I have observed the struggles that students undergo as they attempt to fashion a sense of who they are. On the one hand, they attempt to remain faithful to their past history and to what they have become. On the other hand, they want to explore a newfound sense of selfhood and to experience the possibilities before them.

Among the many selves that adolescents must organize and come to terms with is the experience of who they are morally—or what might be termed the moral self. Moreover, psychologists note that everyone seeks to view himself or herself as a moral person. In spite of what we read about the impulsiveness and materialism of today's youth, the quest for a moral self is central to the adolescent's life experience. Often a young person's behavior may indicate the opposite; his or her concerns may appear far removed from questions of morality. Yet, when we examine the adolescent's situation more closely, we see significant personal struggles and evolving moral questions. Frequently these questions are not articulated clearly (and often must be interpreted from a variety of contradictory behaviors and related questions), but they are there. Psychiatrist Robert Coles captures the essence of youth's moral search when he notes,

> what matters for our young people, finally, is the quality of their home and school life—the origins of the moral character we adults possess or lack. Young Americans in the late 1980s sort themselves out the way young people always have. Those who have been lucky not by dint of their parents' money or power, but their continuous affection and concern, their wish to uphold certain ethical principles and then to live them, rather than merely mouthing them—such youths are well able to handle some of the nonsense and craziness this late part of the twentieth century has managed to offer us all.

My own framework for addressing questions of morality is psychological. By training I am a clinical psychologist. From this vantage point, I believe that aiding young people in developing their moral selves requires careful attention to youth's developmental experiences. In other words, the call to moral growth is a call to transform one's nature (Rom. 8:11), a nature that is best expressed as a complex blend of emotions, perceptions, and thoughts that are distinctly and uniquely experienced at a particular age. Nature influences not only one's ability to hear the Gospel's call, but also one's ability to interpret this call and respond consistently to it. Throughout these pages I place special emphasis on the need to articulate a moral vision that is sensitive to the everyday lives of youth. At the same time, I see a challenge in any moral vision that invites continuing conversion.

The approach I set forth in the following pages can best be termed "pastoral psychology," and it encompasses three dimensions. First, it brings apprecation and sensitivity to the struggles that youth experience. Second, it takes account of the observations and insights offered by leading developmental theorists about the experiences which youth undergo. Third, it emphasizes the use of counseling strategies, particularly the search for insight and thought offered by questioning techniques.

Although a pastoral-psychology approach always needs interaction and dialogue with other disciplines, I believe it offers the optimum strategy for addressing the developmental and pastoral needs of youth. The goal is to provide for them in such a way that their future lives might truly mirror the "hope" to which they are called (1 Pet. 3:15).

Charles Shelton, S.J.
Regis College
Denver, Colorado

CHAPTER ONE

Defining Adolescent Morality

Several years ago I shared with a friend my interest in adolescent morality. I informed him that I was writing a paper for a graduate course on the topic. In an offhanded way my friend replied, "it must be an awfully short paper!" We both had a good laugh.

Afterward, I pondered my friend's reaction. On the surface his response made sense. How often do we link the words *adolescent* and *morality*? Yet as adults we all too often fail to recognize the challenges that adolescence presents to any attempt at forming a moral self. Nonetheless, it is in adolescence that one discovers the capacities and undergoes the experiences necessary for authentic moral choice and commitment. This is not to suggest that the adolescent experience of developing a moral self is a once-for-all affair. On the contrary, acquiring moral maturity is a long and sometimes unpredictable venture in which the adolescent comes to experience himself or herself as a moral person. Not surprisingly, such a developmentally based view of moral growth has significance for youth ministry and religious education.

What Is Adolescent Morality?

Few topics have generated the interest of educators and developmental psychologists as the term *morality*. The waning of public morals in the 1970s during the Vietnam War and the Watergate affair, the demand for "authenticity" and "honesty" in interpersonal relationships, and the questioning of once-sacred values (for example, traditional sex roles and behaviors, or allegiance to political and legal authority) have converged to stimulate debate about what constitutes morality for today's youth.

To examine the meaning of morality for adolescents, we need first to define this developmental period. Characteristically, definitions of adolescence have tended to emphasize one or more dominant feature, such as chronological age, physical maturation, economic independence, or emotional development. We might seek to incorporate all of these dimensions by defining adolescence as

> a chronological period beginning with the physical and emotional processes leading to sexual and psychosocial maturity and ending at an ill-defined time when the individual achieves independence and social productivity. This period is associated with rapid physical, psychological, and social changes.[1]

This definition has several advantages. For one, it incorporates a developmental time frame, that is, it points out that adolescence includes junior and senior high as well as the undergraduate college years. This "ill-defined time," moreover, encompasses a period of ten years (roughly the years from age twelve to twenty-two). The junior-high years are usually referred to as early adolescence while senior high is associated with middle adolescence. College undergraduates are viewed as late adolescents; another term commonly used for this last age group is young adult. Second, this definition also points out the multidimensional factors that define adolescence: economic, emotional, physical, and social factors must be given consideration when describing this age period. And last, it suggests factors which impact on the adolescent's experience: family and society are important factors to consider when exploring adolescence.

Although the word *adolescent* or the developmental period of adolescence might be adequately defined, a much more imposing challenge exists when we attempt to formulate a meaning of morality that relates to the adolescent years. In order to accomplish this, several avenues must be explored. For one, we need to explore in more detail the moral struggles of this age period and the contributions made by contemporary moral psychology to our understanding of adolescent morality. After examining these two areas we will be prepared to offer a perspective on morality that is relevant for the adolescent experience.

The Ebb and Flow of Moral Maturity in Adolescence

Most adults give somewhat ambivalent accounts of their own adolescence. This most likely reflects the acutely felt vicissitudes so characteristic of these developmental years. Rare is the adult who can think of his or her adolescence without recalling feelings of interior joy, moments of dread and fear, and periodic confusion. Why is this so? One answer outweighs almost all others: No other stage of life offers such intensely felt uncertainty. For the adolescent, the security of childhood has yielded to a time of searching and questioning without the corresponding respite of stability and experience that results from the adult's grounding in reflective experience, vocational commitment, and relationships that have borne the test of time. In other words, at least in early and middle adolescence (the junior- and senior-high years), there is little experience of what might be termed morally felt foundations—those experiences that blend psychic attachment and value awareness (more will be said about the meaning of "morally felt foundations" in chapter 3). On a cognitive level, the adolescent is aware of moral rules, yet he or she often lacks a more deeply experienced understanding of the need for and source of these moral utterances. Thus, the lonely adolescent all too often falls prey to the influences of not so well-intentioned peers. The troubled young person seeks solace in stereotypic attitudes. The insecure youth retreats to the world of self-destructive behavior (for example, alcohol and drug abuse). As a consequence, on a conscious level, moral rules are known, but on an experiential level, uncertainties, fears, and insecurities blend to lead the adolescent to engage in damaging and self-defeating behaviors.

In a similar vein, the emotional world of the adolescent is often in disarray; it lacks the firm ground of a guiding and stable perspective. Youth thrive on felt experience. Unfortunately, without a foundation for their affections in stable and secure relational experiences, they surrender to moodiness and often volatile outbursts of feelings. Emotions exercise a critical role in the adolescent's moral experience. Often the defining criterion for morality during this period is how one feels. Unfortunately, emotions are all too often at the mercy of developmental needs and become a vehicle for self-absorption rather than moral clarity.

3

The process of adolescent development that creates such felt uncertainty presents a critical focus for discussion. Many mental health experts have noted that adolescence is not the debilitating "storm and stress" period that so often appears as a cultural stereotype. In fact, evidence indicates that adolescents experience emotional illness at a rate in line with the population as a whole. However, because of cognitive and emotional changes, there is quite often a felt awareness of uncertainty that leads to excessive self-focus and unnecessary introspection. This feeling of uncertainty is not consciously understood by a child, whereas an adult has a longer history of previous experiences that provides the means for dealing with uncertainty.

Factors Impeding Moral Maturity in Secondary School and College-Age Youth

When the Christian speaks of moral growth, there is the explicit recognition of what is "nongrowthful," or what we term "sin." Moralist Timothy O'Connell says that sin only makes sense in the presence of a relationship with God. "Apart from God, in the absence of God, sin is literally meaningless."[2] Sin is a part of the human condition. It is also a personal act that, over time, leads in a direction. Sin portrays one's very existence. It speaks of an inner alienation both from God and from one's brothers and sisters. It points to the false viewpoints that habitually cloud and disorient one's life journey. (There are many definitions of the term *sin*. What we refer to here is personal sin or the adolescent's awareness of actual moral transgressions. Within this context, we view sin as a disruption within the very nature of the person. In other words, the fundamental reality of human life is its relational nature—a relationship with God, self, and others. On all these levels, sin separates the person from what is essential for moral growth.)

What does sin mean for the adolescent? How does the adolescent experience a sense of sinfulness? Though one should address an overall framework for sin, it is imperative that the pastoral minister understand the adolescent "experience" of sin. From my own pastoral work and training as a psychologist I conclude there exist several identifiable aspects of the adolescent experience of sinfulness.

4

The first aspect is a felt lack of integration. Because the adolescent has yet to integrate in an adequate way the ambiguity and complexity of various emotional experiences, he or she can experience "alien" troubled emotions, such as an overly punitive sense of guilt. Correspondingly, because these feelings are not yet integrated, many adolescents (particularly younger adolescents) find difficulty in experiencing the self as "both good and bad," that is, as ambiguous. Lacking integration, some adolescents might focus inordinately on the critical feelings that have been aroused and be blindly absorbed in such feelings. In effect, they experience a sense of "totalism" and blindly accept a sense of worthlessness. This way of coping with sinfulness is most prevalent in the early and middle adolescent years when the adolescent struggles to maintain a sense of self that is coherent. By "coherent" I am referring to a self that can integrate and be comfortable with a variety of self-statements such as "I am a good person," "I am anxious," "I am mistaken when I do some things," "I am happy." Young persons are apt to seize upon one dimension of their feelings and associate this with sin. The most common example of this is the adolescent who feels very guilty over an action and views himself or herself as worthless while ignoring other dimensions of the self that contradict this felt sense of worthlessness. Equally important, however, is the fact that because this lack of integration is so commonplace, many young people will prefer not to focus on a sense of personal sinfulness and prefer to view themselves as omnipotent and downplay or disregard the meaning of sin in their lives. In effect, "totalism" is a defensive strategy that allows the adolescent to experience life with little self-scrutiny.

A second dimension of the adolescent sense of sin is the fragile nature of self-esteem. Often lacking felt experiences of their own self-worth, adolescents will often report personal wrongdoing not only by saying, "I did something wrong," but also, "I am a bad person." In other words, they find difficulty in separating what they do from who they are. Self-reference statements take on a rather denigrating quality that points to the self rather than the behavior.

A final dimension of the adolescent's experience of sin is its relational qualities. The experience of adolescence is the experience of relationships. In some fundamental sense, adolescents not only have relationships, they are their relationships. A sense of sin for the adolescent is often experienced as a sense of estrangement.

There is a felt sense of alienation from God as well as others. This troubled feeling can be tremendously disruptive for the adolescent. Without a sense of bondedness, the adolescent is left adrift and vulnerable to crippling introspection that can be damaging and self-defeating.

Many people wonder about the wisdom of stressing sinfulness with adolescents. Some raise the objection that youth, overwhelmed by developmental insecurities and inner doubts, should not be addressed in the language of "sin." Such a view, however, confuses content and process. It is essential that adults convey the meaning of sinfulness to adolescents in ways filled with compassionate sensitivity and loving guidance. Yet, the very fact of sin needs clear articulation. In short, if we downplay a young person's capacity for sin, we run the risk of depriving the adolescent of the enriching experience of personal forgiveness that is the central reality of Jesus' redemptive message. Youth are ill-served by well-intentioned but misdirected efforts that fail to stress the empowering richness of the Christian mystery of forgiveness.

Formal Thinking

One striking change that occurs in adolescence is a qualitative change in the adolescent's thinking. The thought of the adolescent is markedly distinct from that of the child. During the preadolescent years, the thinking patterns of the child are concrete, whereas in the adolescent years thinking advances beyond the concrete focus to what is known as formal thinking. There are several dimensions of formal thought. First, adolescents are capable of focusing emotionally on their own ideas. This is apparent in the adolescent who is caught up in some type of cause. There is a passionate quality to the adolescent's thinking. At times, one wonders whether the adolescent can even be free of his or her idea since the investment appears so intense and total (as in some cases of adolescent political involvement, for example). In addition, the thinking pattern of the adolescent shows the capacity for abstraction and hypothesizing. In childhood, one is wedded to the concrete situation at hand, but with adolescence, a person begins to conceptualize and think globally in abstract ways. Another characteristic of formal thinking is its introspective nature. Adolescents can appear at times to be lost in their own thought. There is, for many adolescents, an almost incessant self-absorption. In short, some adolescents are overly preoccupied by their own thinking and can appear indifferent to the realities around them. Finally, adolescents are oriented toward the future. This tendency opens the way for adolescent egocentrism. Whereas childhood egocentrism is defined by the child's inability to take the perspective of another, adolescent egocentrism originates in the wedding of adolescent thinking with the adolescent role.

> Moreover, the adolescent manifestation of egocentrism stems directly from the adoption of adult roles, since . . . the adolescent not only tries to adapt his ego to the social environment but, just as emphatically, tries to adjust the environment to his ego. In other words, he begins to think about the society in which he is looking for a place, he has to think about his own future activity and about how he himself might transform this society. The result is a relative failure to distinguish between his own point of view as an individual called upon to organize a life program and the point of view of the group which he hopes to reform.[3]

Because adolescent egocentrism includes a fascination with one's own thought, the realities of the world, in effect, yield to the adolescent's own idealized theories and understandings. Moreover, the adolescent not only adapts the self to adult roles but in an egocentric sense wonders how the views of other individuals and groups can be influenced by his or her own thinking.

Psychologist David Elkind has contributed the most elaborate formulation of adolescent egocentrism. He notes that one of the most discernible qualities of such thinking is adolescents' preoccupation with their own thought. Correspondingly, the adolescent has difficulty differentiating the focus of his or her own thinking from the concerns of others. In effect, this self-focusing nature of adolescent thinking leads him or her to believe mistakenly that others are also preoccupied with his or her thoughts or behaviors. Consequently, the adolescent "thus constructs an imaginary audience that is constantly monitoring his or her own behavior."[4] Unfortunately, this egocentric quality can become what psychologist John Conger terms a "minor tragedy"; that is, this egocentric stance often prevents the adolescent from being aware of the needs and feelings of others.

Elkind offers a "corollary" to the imaginary audience that also originates in the adolescent's egocentrism: the personal fable. If the adolescent finds difficulty in differentiating between his or her own thoughts and the thoughts of others, he or she may develop a mistaken sense of omnipotence or uniqueness. In other words, because others focus on "me," "I" must be someone "special." As a result, a personal fable is constructed. Unfortunately, such thinking often engenders foolish and ill-fated risks whereby the adolescent erroneously views himself or herself as the exception, the one who can disregard rules with impunity.

From the psychoanalytic perspective, the adolescent's absorption in his or her own thinking most likely serves a crucial defensive function. Adolescence can be a time of psychic stress and investment in thought or symbolic or representational imagery (various forms of thinking) can provide a sort of safe attachment, a shield from deeply felt emotional needs.

Formal thinking can prevent the adolescent from being aware of others and can serve as the catalyst for foolish and immature behaviors. Of course, thinking by itself is hardly the cause of this behavior, but it furnishes a basic support for impulsive and selfish action.

Lack of Life Experience

More than in any other phase, the lack of an identity characterizes the adolescent's life experience. Few developmental issues underscore the adolescent's developmental age more than the search for identity. On the one hand, identity acquisition allows the adolescent to develop moral responsibility. On the other hand, the development of a moral self necessitates experimentation with various behaviors in order to experience, literally, what psychically "fits." Haphazard and at times impulsively chosen experimental commitments lead to erratic, foolish, and at times destructive experiences that harm both the adolescent and others. The adolescent who blindly follows the peer group or who sexually "acts out" is often attempting to discover "who I am." With time, as well as with adult sensitivity and challenge, the vast majority of adolescents are able to form a moral identity, though the questions and issues that forge this identity linger long into the young adult years.

Insufficient Reflection

Related to the above is the limited nature of reflective thought so integral for making a moral choice. I have found this to be true for both secondary-school youth as well as the college undergraduate. Unfortunately, adults fail to appreciate the limited depth of the adolescent's reflection. All too often we dialogue with youth as though they could reason and reflect as we do; we fail to recognize the gaps and loosely reasoned statements they make. Lacking a personal life history of well-thought-out moral choices that allow him or her to respond to a variety of dilemmas, the adolescent often succumbs to blinding situational stresses that can eclipse a wider perspective necessary for understanding moral issues.

Peer Approval

A good example of situational stress is the adolescent's tendency to adopt the peer group's standards when encountering a moral question. One of the most convenient ways to separate from parents and define the self as independent is to embrace the lifestyle and behavior of one's peers. More than anything, this adoption of peer standards gives the adolescent the best of all possible worlds. On the one hand, he or she is able to say no to the adult world (thus proclaiming a psychological sense of independence) while on the other hand be absorbed in the security of the peer group (which lessens independence). This latter phenomenon can lead to what is known as the "tyranny of the peer group." In many instances the adolescent is truly unfree, for he or she is at the mercy of peer influence and is psychologically incapable of resisting peer pressure.

We should note here that the stereotype of the adolescent who simply accedes to peer demands is inaccurate. In reality, parents and adolescents are not at odds on most questions. In fact, there exists a remarkable similarity of views between adolescents and their parents on many important issues. A basic rule of thumb is that the more important the issue is to the adolescent's life, the more apt he or she is to seek guidance of parents or other trusted adults. Peer influence over critical issues important to the adolescent is most likely to occur when there is poor communication in the adolescent-parent relationship.

As a rule we can say that almost all adolescents at one time or another are apt to question and challenge adult rules and values. Moreoever, a certain level of questioning and challenge of adult authority is psychologically healthy; that is, an overly controlled adolescent who submits to every adult command with little questioning or challenge is more than likely to develop a less mature sense of self. As a consequence, in adulthood, when significant moral issues and concerns are confronted, there is less ability to respond adequately. Such adolescents (and adults) never really take personal responsibility for their behavior. Rather, they prefer to yield to the authority of others to determine their own moral stance.

Still, peers are an ever-present reality. I vividly recall an adolescent who told me that she was so thankful that her parents insisted that she be home from a party by midnight. She stated that, on her own, she would never have been able to withstand the pressure of her peers and leave the party. Psychologically, this adolescent, unable to assert her moral self, reached for external structures to shield her from peer demands.

In sum, the "tyranny" of the peer group is a double-edged sword. On the one hand, it offers an avenue for the adolescent to establish a healthy sense of independence. On the other hand, it proves a tempting invitation to escape responsibility and the challenging demands of moral maturity.

Inconsistency

Adolescent behaviors often exhibit a wide variety of inconsistencies. James Fowler relates this to what he calls "compartmentalizing."[5] Thus, adolescents are prone to act one way with parents and another way with peers. In effect, the adolescent compartmentalizes his or her life according to what role is currently being called upon. Utilizing roles is the best way to categorize this phenomenon. In some sense, adolescence can be depicted as the "battle of roles." Thus, an adolescent is a son or daughter, student, athlete, friend, club member, brother or sister, worker, and so on. A listing of these roles highlights the potential for role conflicts and, correspondingly, the all too commonplace discrepant behaviors that accompany these diverse roles. Many adolescents continually engage in contradictory behaviors without really attending to the discrepancies that exist among various life roles. Thus an adolescent behaves one way at school, another way at work, and so on. These various contradictions occur because a cohesive sense of self-identity has not yet been achieved. Only with a maturing sense of identity, of "who I really am," is the adolescent capable of with-standing various pressures and behaving in a consistent fashion across a variety of roles.

Risk Taking

The above features point to a phenomenon in adolescence that is a growing concern to mental health experts—the adolescent ten-dency for taking risk. Health psychologist Nancy Adler states, "the immediate experience is what matters to them, not worries about long-term consequences."[6] Adolescents focus on the here and now. They often do not see the results their own actions have on them-selves as well as others. Adolescents lack an adult's frame of refer-ence. In other words, they are deficient in the depth of experience that provides a template for assessing and comprehending the con-sequences of their personal actions. Correspondingly, lacking a frame of reference as well as a firm sense of their own identity, they fill this void by adopting the tacit rules and norms of the peer group. The difficulty with this peer frame of reference is that the group action is often no more informed than their own unreflected responses.

Modeling

The cognitive changes that transpire during adolescence allow the young person to think critically about adult standards and be-haviors. With the shedding of simplistic childhood notions, the ad-olescent often begins a critical examination of adults. Inevitably, the adolescent discovers that adults fail to live up to their own pro-fessed standards. Some adolescents view these adult inconsistencies as hypocritical. This realization, in turn, engenders disillusionment and negativity. The fact that many adults fail to be good Christian role models becomes for some youth a justification of their own less than ideal behaviors. The adolescent sometimes seems to walk a tightrope between youthful idealism and cynicism, the former nur-tured by the optimism focused on an adult world yet to be experi-enced, the latter fueled by disappointment over the lack of adult models.

Relativity

Cognitive and emotional changes during adolescence force a re-evaluation of once-sacred childhood beliefs. The unquestioned statements of parents or other significant adults are no longer accepted. What emerges is a profoundly new experience. To one degree or another, relativity (or the continual questioning of what is accepted) becomes the norm. This shift from certainty to ambiguity can create a period of moral crisis. In order to temper this newly experienced doubt some adolescents regress from serious examination and retreat to an uncritical and rigid acceptance of parental standards. In other words, some adolescents foreclose the exploration of their own moral selves and seek safety in parental wishes and beliefs.

Other adolescents, usually in the late-adolescence phase, adopt a philosophical view of life that dispels insecurities and doubts by providing intellectually coherent answers. Still other adolescents entertain a variety of beliefs as they attempt to develop some type of personal meaning for their lives. Finally, some youth avoid altogether any serious confrontation with moral concerns; these adolescents, in other words, call a "time out" from moral examination and are satisfied with current (and often desultory) activities and pursuits. This group of adolescents take a rather unfocused approach to their own identity search. These adolescents often become preoccupied in what appear to be aimless activities that lack purpose or meaningful goals.

Most adolescents, however, make some effort at moral scrutiny. What occurs in the midst of their self-evaluation is a sense of relativity, uncertainty, and questioning. The adolescent in the midst of his or her own life changes and newly experienced intellectual abilities discovers that relativity is the "true" world perspective. Indeed, this newly developed insight blends with the perceived pluralism and moral ambiguity that are held up as the cultural norm.[7] In effect, the combination of relativity and pluralism leads many adolescents to identify truth solely in terms of subjective experience (what is right is simply decided by the individual). The adolescent comes to believe that what is moral depends upon a person's own life goals and realistic possibilities. The adolescent's assumption is, Who is to decide what is right? This perceived moral

12

relativity leads to a moral subjectivism that is shaped by developmental needs. All in all, the ever-present reality of relativity is one of the major challenges for adolescents as they fashion the meaning of a moral self.

Sense of Powerlessness

The adolescent's social role leaves little room for a sense of active mastery. Though they are no longer children, they are unable to bring about a stable sense of control over their lives. Often adolescents act in inappropriate ways out of personal frustration and a sense of inadequacy. The roots of this inadequacy are social rather than personal; that is, they result from the sense many adolescents have of their own powerlessness to alter effectively their environment or to bring about their wishes. Some adolescents are quite enterprising in this regard and can channel their need for self-mastery into socially constructive pursuits, achievements, or hobbies that bring them status and recognition. However, many adolescents lack either the forums, personal talents, or ingenuity to bring about such mastery and self-completion. Consequently, such adolescents are tempted to act out occasionally in order simply to have others acknowledge their own need for recognition and some sense of personal power.

Culture

One area recently receiving attention in moral education is the imposing presence of cultural and societal factors that influence the adolescent's moral life. The psychic numbing occasioned by nuclear war threats, the alienation fostered by competition, and the insidious lure of a consumer-oriented culture are difficult to combat. Youth today, facing an uncertain economic future, are vulnerable to the trappings offered by a materialistic society. The realities of cultural influences have forced adults to realize they can no longer simply encourage youth to be "moral." What is needed are environments where young people can discuss, dialogue, and share their common concerns and doubts. It is unrealistic for adults to expect youth to develop a mature moral self if they are not provided opportunities to share and discuss questions. (At the same time, I have become uneasy with the simplistic notions so evident in some of today's social justice education. All too often literature for adolescents speaks in dichotomous terms about violence-peace or justice-injustice without giving adequate attention to complex national or international realities.) Adolescents have the right to hear that there are many sides to complex issues and that men and women of goodwill might legitimately disagree on what particular end is best for achieving a socially just solution. Furthermore, such simplistic portrayals of issues disregard the very basic developmental experience of the adolescent, who has a more complex view of the world · through his or her growing cognitive maturity. For example, the question of a dual minimum wage for the adolescent is an issue of great relevance for youth today because it involves their own economic livelihood. Yet, numerous people who profess various religious beliefs can be found on all sides of this question. Can one truly say that there is a "Christian" position on this issue? There has evolved over the past few decades a large body of writing on the Christian response to major social issues, such as nuclear war and the American economy, that provide a resource for the Christian in a complex society. Yet, in helping adolescents develop a moral sense of these issues, we must cautiously allow them to explore both the complexities of these issues as well as the various interpretations Christians give to them.

Some Questions

In sum, there are numerous competing influences that impact on the adolescent's moral life. Below are questions that should prove helpful for the religious educator or youth minister. Obviously, one need not try to cover many of these areas at once with the adolescent. I have found it most helpful to concentrate on one or two specific areas and reflect with the adolescent on various aspects of his or her life experience.

The reader is encouraged to vary and to expand on the questions listed. These or other questions can often serve the basis for the development of a fruitful dialogue with the adolescent. In general, more abstract questions are best used with middle and late adolescents. Concrete examples are always helpful to focus the adolescent on the theme of the question.

Formal thinking: Are you aware of all aspects of the situation before acting (it is helpful here to focus on a specific situation that is of interest to the adolescent)? Are there ways in which you see yourself as invincible? Are there situations or events where you feel pressured to engage in a certain action because you feel others might be watching you? To what extent do you respond simply to the emotion present in the situation?

Lack of life experience: When you think about the word *moral*, what comes to mind? What initiatives have you taken personally to live this definition? How would you relate this definition to your current life? How does your definition of the word "moral person" differ from a few years ago? What key events or significant people have shaped your view of what it means to be moral?

Insufficient reflection: Who would you name as the people who most influence your life? What is it about each of these people that makes them influential in your life? When making decisions, in what areas of your life do you find yourself more impulsive? More reflective? Do you have times and places where you can reflect? What kind of a place (setting) do you need in order to reflect?

Peer approval: Who are your friends? Why is each of these people your friend? What values do you share with each of these friends? In what ways are you like your friends? In what ways are you not like your friends (or a particular friend)? Do you need to feel yourself part of a peer group all the time? What values does your peer group share? How comfortable are you with taking a stand different from your peer group? How do you define friendship? What do you look for in a friend?

Inconsistency: Can you identify the roles in your life? What are the values important for you in each of these roles? Are there some values that are important for you regardless of the role? What are they? How do you handle conflict between two roles? To what extent are your values different in the various roles? Why might this be so? Are there roles in which it is hard for you to be yourself or to be the way you would really like to be? Is some part of you living a "false self"?

Risk taking: Are there things you do just for a thrill? Do you sometimes push things to the limit? How do you think these actions might affect or possibly even harm others or yourself? Do you have a "need" to take risks? How often do you ask yourself what might happen if you do this?

Modeling: Who are the heroes in your life? Who are the people that you most admire? Why do you value these people? Who do you wish to be like? What values do these people hold which you would like to have?

Relativity: What are the values that guide your life? If you had to rank these values which would be ranked the highest? What types of dilemmas in your life do you have difficulty in resolving? Can you give an example? How do you show respect to individuals who might differ from your way of thinking? How well do you tolerate ideas that are different from yours?

Sense of powerlessness: Do you sometimes do some things just to have an effect? What in your life have you really achieved or done to give you a sense of accomplishment? Can you take pride in what you do without being overbearing or boastful? At the same time, can you feel really good about yourself when you do accomplish something?

Culture: What do you believe are the goals and major priorities of our culture? How are these goals similar and different from your own goals? What do you see as the "good" things about American culture? What would you change about American culture if you could?

Moral Development Theory and Adolescent Morality

Over the past two decades, the study of morality's meaning has proven a fruitful area for research. This endeavor has brought together the thinking of philosophers, psychologists, educators, and theologians. This convergence of disciplines has created a wide and diverse assortment of definitions regarding how morality develops. Among the various theorists who have addressed the issue of moral development, none approaches the significance of Lawrence Kohlberg.[8]

The impetus for Kohlberg's work comes from his disenchantment with what he termed the "bag of virtues" approach to morality. Essentially, the "bag of virtues" approach stressed that traditional values such as honesty, altruism, and self-control could

16

be taught and that these values were valid indicators of morality in every culture. In other words, there existed a traditional set of values and behaviors that all people could endorse. Kohlberg refused to accept this more traditional view of morality. He stated that the virtue approach to morality was inadequate. For one, individuals in different cultures adopt various values. Also, an individual would not necessarily behave morally in all situations: one might be, for example, honest in one situation and act dishonestly in the same situation the next day or in a similar situation; the child might cheat in one class but behave in an exemplary fashion in another class. Often, said Kohlberg, the setting or environment influences how one behaves.

In order to rectify the situational relativism so pervasive in the "bag of virtues" approach, Kohlberg developed a theory of morality based on his study of subjects in late childhood and adolescence. His theory is the most conceptually integrated and empirically tested of all moral development theories.

Kohlberg maintains that one's understanding of justice is the most significant factor in understanding morality. He states that "there is a natural sense of justice intuitively known by the child."[9] With development, a person alters his or her thinking as to what constitutes justice. Kohlberg documented through his studies a six-stage theory of moral development with each stage representing a different understanding of justice. Kohlberg maintains that one passes through the stages in a given order and that one does not skip stages. Through numerous studies in many cultures, including the United States, Israel, Turkey, Kohlberg claims a universal grounding for his theory.

In order to measure the advancement of moral reasoning, Kohlberg presented his subjects with hypothetical situations called "moral dilemmas." For each of these situations, the subject was instructed to provide "reasons" for the behavior of the character in the dilemma. A well-known example is the famous Heinz dilemma. In this dilemma, the subject discovers that Heinz's wife was near death from cancer. A local druggist had discovered a drug that could cure Heinz's wife, but was charging the customers ten times the actual cost of the drug. Unable to either borrow enough money or cajole the druggist into lowering the price, Heinz thought about stealing the drug. After reading the Heinz story, the subject then responds to a series of questions exploring the reasons for advocating a certain course of action for the character. The subject's responses can be subsumed under one of the six stages (or various substages). The stages are briefly summarized below.

Preconventional Level

The dominant influences at the preconventional level of moral reasoning are the external demands of authority and the child's own hedonistic orientation toward pleasure and away from pain.

The punishment-and-obedience orientation (stage one):   Moral reasoning at stage one uses the criterion of avoiding punishment to determine right from wrong. At this stage, the child is dependent upon others. The preoccupation of moral reasoning, therefore, is to deter punishment and avoid the adverse consequences of one's actions.

The instrumental-relativist orientation (stage two):   At stage two, the child is more concerned with personal needs and desires. The child determines whether something is right or wrong on the basis of personal desires and only infrequently on the basis of the needs of others. At this stage, the child might do something for another, but some reciprocity is expected. In other words, reciprocity becomes a matter of "you scratch my back and I'll scratch yours."

Conventional Level

At the conventional level, the young person is increasingly aware of the external demands of various groupings—family, school, government, society—that begin to make demands on him or her. This awareness of others is concretized in loyalty and "conformity" to groups, one's nation, and the current social order. The young person respects and uses others as reference points in his or her reasoning about the rightness and wrongness of personal acts. This level emerges in later childhood and early adolescence. Most adolescents and adults are found to reason at this level.

The good boy–nice girl orientation (stage three):   At stage three, the person is motivated by the desire to gain the acceptance and approval of others. Conformity is prized, and personal actions are planned to meet with the acceptance and social approval of the person's own group. The individual places value on conforming types of behavior. The behavior of others tends to be evaluated by intention ("He or she means well"). Being "nice" becomes the norm for earning the approval of others.

The law-and-order orientation (stage four): At stage four, the person places a high emphasis on "law and order." A person's duty within the social environment becomes increasingly important. Rules are prized, and authority is given greater respect. The individual believes that right or wrong correspond to "doing one's duty," that is, fulfilling the demands made on the individual by observing the law and performing expected socially sanctioned behaviors.

Postconventional Level

An individual who obtains the postconventional level of moral reasoning begins to prize values that exist independently of groups and the culture. He or she recognizes universalizing moral principles that are followed for their own sake. At this level, the person's moral principles are focused on higher values such as equality and justice for all. Right and wrong are determined according to these universal principles.

The social contract-legalistic orientation (stage five): At stage five, the person realizes that law is for the common good of all, that laws protect the rights and welfare of all members of society. He or she sees that although conflicts between individuals and the law can exist, the law must prevail because the generalized acceptance of this law promotes the welfare of all. At the same time, the individual who is at this stage of development, unlike the person who is at stage four, perceives law as a benefit to the common good; laws are, therefore, not rigid, but rather are subject to alteration in order to meet changing human needs.

The universal-ethical principle orientation (stage six): At stage six, the individual uses universal principles to determine the morality of personal acts. Of particular importance are ethical principles that are derived from the individual's personal conscience and that have universal application (for example, equality or justice). The law is still thought to be important, but there are higher values that deserve human allegiance.

The individual's advancement in Kohlberg's theory shows a movement away from self-absorption (preconventional) toward an awareness of the thinking and the feeling of others (conventional). Finally, attention is given to universal moral principles that respect the rights of all human beings. At the first level, the primary concern is the self. At the second level, the individual's growth outward leads to greater respect for law and for society's demands. Finally, at the third level, universal moral principles that prize justice and equality toward all men and women are fostered through principled moral reasoning.[10]

Kohlberg's view of adolescent moral reasoning has been in a state of ongoing revision. The alteration in Kohlberg's thinking on adolescent morality is best viewed by examining Kohlberg's now classic (and idyllic) article that portrayed the adolescent's moral experience, "The Adolescent as Philosopher: The Discovery of Self in a Postconventional World." In this article, Kohlberg relates the adolescent's struggle to find meaning within a society whose norms and values the adolescent increasingly questions. This period of doubt and reevaluation sows the seeds and sets the stage for advancement to postconventional (principled) moral thinking.

> The postconventional level is first evident in adolescence and is characterized by a major thrust toward autonomous moral principles which have validity and application apart from authority of the groups of persons who hold them and apart from the individual's identification with those persons or groups.[11]

Kohlberg recognized that the acquisition of formal thinking created a fertile field for the transition to truly principled thinking; indeed, Kohlberg consistently maintained that postconventional thinking was impossible without the presence of formal thought. A key to this transition is the adolescent's experience of relativism which allows for the questioning of society's norms and values while he or she was still uncommitted to moral principles. Moreover, in his early work Kohlberg viewed the adolescent's questioning and rejection of conventional understandings of justice as allied with the growing mass social movements that critically challenged American cultural norms (for example, protest movements in the late sixties).

In contrast to this optimistic view of the advancement of moral reasoning, Kohlberg, by the late seventies, stated that postconventional thinking was possible only with the passing of the adolescent years. In an article published in 1980, "Educating for a Just Society: An Updated and Revised Statement," Kohlberg no longer viewed adolescence as the harbinger for postconventional thought. He saw high school youth as wedded to conventional thinking. Kohlberg stated:

> In summary, my 1976 lecture on education for justice stressed a retrenchment from my 1968 Platonic stage 6 to a stage 5 goal and conception of justice. The present paper reports a further retrenchment to stage 4 goals as the ends of civic education. It discusses my civic educational efforts for the last four years at Cambridge high school's alternative Cluster School. Our Cluster approach is not merely Socratic and developmental, it is indoctrinative. Its goal is not attainment of the fifth stage but a solid attainment of the fourth stage commitment to being a good member of a community or a good citizen.[12]

Kohlberg and his followers have most recently given great priority to the importance of a communal atmosphere where students actually experience a sense of justice in peer and teacher-student relationships. A community for Kohlberg represents a forum for shared decision making, thereby allowing students the opportunity to experience firsthand issues of justice. This community also provides opportunities for the discussion of conflicting arguments as well as exposure to more advanced levels of moral reasoning. This emphasis on "community" might well be one of Kohlberg's greatest contributions for it underscores the necessity of a supportive and nurturing environment which sustains the adolescent's moral search. Kohlberg and his associates have reported success in developing moral reasoning in such a communal atmosphere. He now views principled moral thinking as beyond the reach of secondary school youth. For such thinking to take place, students are in need of ongoing life experiences that challenge them to reexamine their own beliefs and invest themselves in deepening commitments (for example, leaving home, making a vocational commitment).

To understand Kohlberg's theory it is important to note several elements. First Kohlberg centers his view of morality on reasoning

21

about justice. In effect, morality for Kohlberg is heavily cognitive. What determines one's level of moral development is how one reasons about justice. Second, because Kohlberg is interested in moral reasoning he does not emphasize the behaviors which flow from this reasoning. This does not mean they are unimportant, and in his later writings Kohlberg focuses more attention on actual behavior; nonetheless, the significant component for Kohlberg's view of morality is how one reasons and not what one does. Likewise, Kohlberg's concern for reasoning about justice leads him to avoid direct reference to content or traditions that faith communities endorse. Kohlberg subscribes to a universal theory of morality based on the centrality of justice which all reasonable people endorse. To focus on the content of one's belief, on the norms of a faith community, would undermine the universality of his theory. That various faith traditions hold differing tenets and values would subvert a universal notion of justice. It should be pointed out that Kohlberg has shown a sensitive ear in listening to the voices of his critics. Accordingly, in order to incorporate the moral concerns of faith communities he has spoken of a stage seven which is specifically oriented to address issues of faith.

When I first read Kohlberg's theory in the midseventies I was intrigued, but I did not believe that his thinking could be reconciled with a Christian view of morality without serious qualification. There are three essential reasons why Christian educators must approach Kohlberg's view of morality with caution.

First, Kohlberg's highly cognitive view of morality leaves too little room for emotion. I seriously doubt that one can deal with pastoral dilemmas or moral concerns in everyday life without giving significant priority to the place of emotions. Emotions have a way of energizing the moral commitments we make. They foster an enduring sense of commitment to the values we prize as central to the moral life. At the same time, emotions also distort and cloud our view of essential moral issues. They often trigger impulsive or defensive reactions rather than provide moral clarity. In this sense, emotions are a double-edged sword. This is easily brought home in examining the life of the adolescent. An adolescent might become passionately involved in a moral cause and use his attraction to some commitment as a way to fuel his concern and sensitivity. Yet, this same adolescent might feel anxious and insecure in relationships and defensively react to another or behave in a manipulative fashion. In other words, thinking about a value or reasoning to a solution is not enough. What is needed is a serious examination of the emotions and how they orient one to behave morally or inhibit the fostering of moral growth.

Second, Kohlberg's view of morality is far removed from the practical realities that confront peoples' everyday lives. There arises legitimate concern as to what degree Kohlberg's hypothetical dilemmas can actually be applied to the concrete everyday world of youth. The well-known Heinz dilemma, where Heinz had to reason whether he should or should not steal a drug from a greedy druggist in order to save his wife's life, provides a good example of this point. This dilemma, as so many of Kohlberg's dilemmas, arises out of conflicts over life-and-death issues and rules of law. Yet, how practical are such dilemmas in the everyday lives of adolescents? Because these dilemmas are so far removed from the everyday lives of young people, adolescents are apt to answer at a higher level than they would if reasoning about more practical everyday issues like how to treat a friend or whether to cheat on a test. A reason for this discrepancy arises out of the adolescent's emotional investment in his or her life situation. One can see in this situation the influence of emotion: adolescents are apt to reason at a lower level when faced with everyday dilemmas because the self is more involved in these concrete dilemmas whereas life-and-death dilemmas are far removed from the adolescent's experience. In other words, the less one is invested in an experience (as with life-and-death situations and rules of law), the more apt one is to endorse lofty moral principles for they provide less opportunity for actual involvement.

Third, there needs to be a clear articulation in any Christian morality of content; this point is critical for the Christian faith community. There must be an articulation of specific content and behavior as morally acceptable and expected of faith believers. Although a given situation might lead to legitimate disagreement and questioning about what approach is morally correct, nonetheless, there are general themes that believers can subscribe to and that must have priority when attempting to present a moral response to a given situation. In this respect, Christian morality does not exist in a vacuum. Rather, there is specific content that is reflected upon and discussed and which becomes a guiding force in the Christian's decision making. This is critically important for the adolescent's discovery of the moral self. That is, the adolescent is often burdened by an intense introspection which leads to an unduly focused sense of self. This preoccupation eclipses significant objective criteria which provide guiding principles for one's action.

Defining an Adolescent Morality

We are now in a position to define a more expansive view of morality that is sensitive to the moral concerns of youth and that facilitates moral growth. Previously, I had argued for a view of morality that takes account of the adolescent's developmental level.[13] I would now like to offer a vision of adolescent morality that incorporates the various facets of adolescent growth. Adolescent morality can be defined as *the adolescent's personal striving, in the midst of his or her own developmental struggles, to internalize and commit the self to ideals within a situational context that incorporates the interplay of the developmental level, the concrete situation, and environmental factors, and which in turn leads to self-maintaining and consistent thoughts, attitudes, and actions.* With this definition we are focusing on the adolescent within the educational context so as to inquire how the adolescent can best acquire moral ideals and continue to grow in these ideals through the passage toward mature Christian adulthood.

An analogy might be helpful in sorting out the advantages of this broadened definition. Psychologist Arnold Lazarus, in *The Practice of Multi-Modal Therapy,* his provocative analysis of psychotherapeutic practice, argues that a one-dimensional understanding of clients in therapy is inadequate.[14] In other words, the therapist is ill-advised to frame his or her treatment of the person seeking help in terms of a specific cognitive, behavioral, biological, or other type of limited therapeutic intervention. Rather, what is needed, says Lazarus, is a broadened framework that incorporates the multiple dimensions of the client's experience. As an answer to this need, Lazarus presents the acronym BASIC ID. This stands for: behavior, affects, sensations, interpersonal relations, cognitions, imagery, and drugs or biological concerns. Only with this more expansive framework can the therapist really hope to meet adequately the needs of the client.

With the definition of morality presented above, I am attempting to incorporate a broadened focus that allows the optimum possibility for adolescent commitment to the ideals of his or her faith community. Utilizing Lazarus's approach, I would like to present the acronym NAPSEME. This acronym represents seven basic orientations that must be addressed for a full understanding of adolescent morality. These seven orientations are: normative, attentive, processing, situational, efficacy, maintaining, and environmental.

Below is a discussion of each of these orientations.

Normative Orientation

James Fowler has defined faith development in terms of a dynamic, active process which does not emphasize specific content or belief. We have already noted above the absence of normative content for Kohlberg's stage development theory. Clearly, however, we can argue that the commitment to religious belief entails ideals and moral norms. In terms of a Christian moral vision, the Decalogue, the Sermon on the Mount, Paul's exhortation on the fruits of the Spirit (Gal. 5:22), as well as a personal experience of Jesus Christ form a valuable template for the adolescent's journey toward moral growth. The challenge for the adolescent resides in personally appropriating these ideals into internal and behavioral commitments as he or she encounters a growing and seemingly complex and relativistic world. It is this commitment to the norms of the faith community in the midst of relativism that fashions the adolescent's maturing moral response.

Attentive Orientation

In order for moral decisions to be made, the adolescent must comprehend and be perceptually aware of the diverse environmental and relational concerns that surround his or her life. For example, an adolescent who is attempting to develop a moral stance in the area of social justice must cognitively assess numerous and multidimensional issues. Further, he or she must be capable of perceiving various social injustices and the multilayered interconnections of cultural and social influences that underlie these injustices. At the same time, there exist developmental inadequacies that work against realizing these social concerns. Adolescents may lack the formal thinking that is necessary for passionate commitment to abstract notions such as peace and equality. An adolescent's stereotypic response may be a response of defensiveness as the young person attempts to balance a striving for independence with the fears that emerge from contact with different groups of people. On an interpersonal level, an adolescent's manipulation and exploitation of another adolescent may prevent a recognition of his or her partner's hurts and fears, even when they are expressed and made obvious. This concept of developmental limitations can help point out the fragile perceptual and cognitive base for many adolescent behaviors inasmuch as many young people are unaware of the numerous issues and personal demands that often frustrate and limit authentic moral choosing.

Processive Orientation.

Developmental theorists such as Erikson, Fowler, and Kohlberg have defined distinctive stages that incorporate unique needs and perspectives. These particular periods might be imaged as filters through which the adolescent attempts to make authentic moral choices. Several essential issues emerge when analyzing the processive nature of adolescent moral decision making. For one, the adolescent in the midst of an identity quest might opt for the values of a particular group (usually the peer group), thereby challenging parental authority; in effect, the adolescent takes on the trappings of a "negative identity." A negative identity is the adolescent's attempt to construct an identity based on behaviors contrary and challenging to adult authority. In other words, the adolescent self comes about through oppositional behavior. Similarly, James Fowler observes that a classic defensive ploy of the adolescent is selectively to choose a definite role such as the member of a particular group and give such priority to that role so as to exclude the necessary behaviors demanded by other roles such as son or daughter, athlete, or friend to a student outside the peer group.[15] Finally, Kohlberg has observed that the regressive tendencies that so afflict youth often lead to a morality of the individual in which the common response becomes "do your own thing, and let others do theirs."[16]

In addition to various behaviors that adolescents display, there also exists an expenditure of psychic energy that is a function of age. Consequently, many adolescents might interpret reality and behavior to suit their own developmental needs. Thus, early adolescents (junior high) are typically preoccupied with rapid physical changes. Middle adolescents (senior high) focus on identity issues and will construe meanings according to this identity quest. College students or late adolescents will seek the solace of intimacy while still constructing their own personal self. If moral growth is to be a central component of religious education, then the thrust of educational endeavors must be sensitive to the actual experiences of youth and the attending behaviors that arise from youth's developmental limitations.

Situational Orientation

As we have noted, commitment to moral norms in the adolescent years are made in the midst of increasing relativity and ambiguity. The adolescent gradually discovers that his or her attempts at commitment to ideals must be subjected to both the criticism and challenge of others as well as the realities of a complex world. Indeed, for Piaget this interaction is critical to the adolescent's intellectual maturation.

In order to appreciate the importance of this orientation I would like to return once again to the quandary an adolescent might encounter when attempting a moral response to the question of a dual minimum wage. A junior in secondary school is faced with the issue of whether to support a dual minimum wage law that might help alleviate some of the scandalous unemployment among youth in this country, particularly among minorities. Although fortunate to have a job, this adolescent has several friends who are either unable to find part-time work or who are underemployed. This is an especially acute problem during the summer months since many of the student's friends are saving for college. Initially this student is quite attracted by the possibilities of finding work opportunities offered through a dual minimum wage. The student realizes that one of the immediate advantages might be a significant increase in the number of jobs available to teenagers. But from a classroom discussion and additional research the student realizes that unscrupulous employers might take advantage of such a system, and that students who already have jobs might experience a lowering of their summer wages. In addition, because of distinctive cultural and economic conditions, a dual wage might not really make a difference in the student's geographic area. Still, the student is highly unsatisfied with the current situation and has even heard a friend's father say that if the minimum wage were not so high, he would be able to employ more summer help. In this complex situation numerous variables compete to make difficult the adolescent's attempt to arrive at a moral stance. Numerous other examples can be gathered that range from the adolescent's attempt to work out a mutuality of rights and duties within a beginning friendship to the late adolescent's attempts at gathering all pertinent information to arrive at a moral position on the draft or nuclear arms. To appreciate the adolescent's growing realization of situational complexity in moral decision making is a task of great consequence for religious education today.

Efficacy Orientation

Moral actions are accomplished by moral agents. This statement implies the capacity to bring about desired outcomes. Just as ideals must be acknowledged and commitments made, so too must factors that aid in implementing these commitments be assessed. This is especially pertinent for adolescents on the road to adulthood. Self-mastery skills, a sense of inner control, positive self-esteem, and development of personal talents and interests are all essential ingredients for promoting a sense of self-efficacy in adolescence. The wondering adolescent who lacks inner control easily falls prey to the external influences of not so well-intentioned peers. The adolescent who desires to dialogue with local merchants about a pressing social-justice issue will most likely experience frustration if the school has not provided adequate human relations training and promoted a positive self-regard which, in effect, allows the student to venture outward to dialogue about personal moral commitments.

Maintaining Orientation

Moral growth is not just applicable to a situation; moral maturity is viewed in terms of the person's capacity to sustain moral behavior over time. Recent findings in psychological research document the numerous possibilities for the development of caring behaviors and positive relationships that reflect Christian values. Among the most exciting discoveries is the fostering of empathy that serves as a catalyst for the development of altruistic behavior. The nurturance of an empathic sense might well constitute the human foundation for the development and growth of Christian praxis.[17]

In addition to the development of empathy, numerous other possibilities exist for maintaining caring behaviors in adolescence. Among those possibilities are articulating values that encourage the development of a distinctive set of behaviors, encouraging the acceptance of personal responsibility among students, allowing opportunities for experiential learning (this is especially helpful if the situation focuses on experiences of human pain and suffering), and providing role-playing opportunities for students in order that they might experience the actual feelings of others who are suffering.

Environmental Orientation

Making moral choices always arises within the context of an environment. Among all the orientations, this one has received little attention from religious educators. Kohlberg has noted that the school is a pivotal force for advancing civic virtue and moral reasoning. James Gustafson talks of a community of "moral discourse" where issues and moral concerns can be discussed and support given the young person who is attempting to understand various moral issues and their consequences. Gerald Grant terms the private school as "both a symbolic and an actual representation of valued moral and intellectual goods."[18]

In a recent discussion regarding the school's "moral function," Jerome Kagan states,

> I believe the schools can play an ameliorative role by providing opportunities for adolescents to persuade themselves of their virtue through acts whose benevolent consequences are not so dependent upon chance, the vicissitudes of peer and adult opinion, or the relative competences of others.[19]

Among the critical "dimensions of character" that Kagan views as important for schools are: "kindness, restraint on aggression, honesty, and a reasonable blend of pride and humility."[20] Clearly, schools need to contend with the issue of what their educational mission is and how they articulate their values to the adolescents they instruct.

The above perspective of adolescent morality has several important features. First, it is interactional; it appreciates both the adolescent self-in-transition as well as the environment in which the adolescent self interacts. Second, this approach is developmental; there is sensitivity shown to the numerous issues that are interwoven throughout these developing years. Third, a positive thrust is stressed; that is, influences and values that sustain and nurture behaviors and caring stances toward others are actively pursued. Fourth, this approach encourages a holistic perspective; in other words, the adolescent self, the environment, and the pertinent issues which occupy the adolescent's attention are all accorded focused attention as youth attempt exploratory, tentative, and enduring moral commitments.

A Check List

Adopting this perspective of morality allows us to appreciate the multiple tasks of adolescents and the struggles they experience as well as the multidimensional features of a well-developed understanding of morality. As a way to summarize this perspective, the following checklist of questions is offered.

Normative orientation: Do the ideals of this educational institution profess for the adolescent valued commitments that speak of sacrifice, compassion, and the value of human life? Is emphasis given to the priority of values? Are these values related in turn to the actual decisions that adolescents experience?

Attentive orientation: Is the adolescent "enlightened" by this educational experience? That is, is the young person provided the opportunity to develop the discerning capacity to define, clarify, and evaluate the numerous issues and complexities of various moral problems and dilemmas?

Processive orientation: Are attempts to educate youth sensitive to the developmental stages out of which young people interact? Does the school present the adolescent with a challenging atmosphere that encourages future growth?

Situational orientation: Can this school experience relate the adolescent's moral ideals and commitments with his or her actual experience? Are there opportunities available for adolescents to work through ambiguous and complex issues and dilemmas and to realize through these undertakings how personal moral commitments might be actualized? Are adults available to offer reflective feedback that might aid the adolescent in dealing with confusion and ambiguity?

Efficacy orientation: Does the school attend to all dimensions of the adolescent's life? Are attempts made to prepare the adolescent for future adult interactions, and are relationship skills part of this training? Through this education does the adolescent gain a deepening understanding of what it means to be an adult?

Maintaining orientation: Is the adolescent provided occasions for experiencing and channeling compassion and sensitivity into types of behavior that reflect deep care and concern for others?

Environmental orientation: What is the "climate" of care and challenge present in this school? Does this school atmosphere answer not only the question of "who I am" but also the deeper moral question of "what am I about?" Are the faculty, administrators, and students aware of and sensitive to the values that this school professes? Are opportunities available to periodically reflect on these values?

A commonly accepted axiom of education is that knowledge is best expressed by noting its integrative and relational qualities. Within this perspective, it would appear that adolescent morality finds a welcome ally. Only through this total viewing of the adolescent-environment interaction can there develop a multidimensional approach that is sensitive to both the adolescent self and the continual challenge of moral commitment.

CHAPTER TWO

A Psychological Model
for Adolescent Morality

In chapter 1 we examined a multidimensional approach to adolescent morality which sought to incorporate all facets of the adolescent experience. In short, we viewed adolescent morality as requiring examination of the ideals of the faith community, appreciating the developmental level of the adolescent, and acknowledging the critical role that environmental factors exercised in the adolescent's moral quest. We turn now to an understanding of morality in the adolescent years that focuses on the essential ingredients of moral choice. We have already viewed the limitations of Kohlberg's theory for morality. A more promising understanding of morality is found in the writing of psychologist James Rest. We will provide a short summary of his theory. After this discussion a Christian model will be offered for the theory that Rest outlines.

Rest's Four Components of Morality

James Rest argues that no current theory incorporates all relevant features that are needed for a thorough understanding of morality, so he formulated the term to include nearly all relevant dimensions.[1] Rest maintains that "we need to attempt a fuller . . . more integrated picture of morality and to envision how the part processes are organized."[2] Rest notes that

> the four components are not presented as four virtues that make up an ideal person; rather they are the major units of analysis in tracing how a particular course of action was produced in the context of a particular situation.[3]

Morality is simply too complex a construct to be subsumed under any one theory. Moreover, morality is a broad construct in which several perspectives must be explored. An adequate theory of morality must look simultaneously at individual persons, their beliefs, and those factors that encourage moral responses as well as those experiences that sustain moral commitment over time. In this regard, the model that Rest develops incorporates the numerous dimensions set forth in the first chapter. From a psychological perspective, as the reader might note, this more elaborated view of morality incorporates more than developmental psychology, the discipline most closely allied with moral psychology. Rest views social influences as well as the environment as integral to the forming of any coherent view of morality. In order to give greater clarity to his thinking, Rest has categorized all aspects of morality into four components.[4] Only by addressing these components, says Rest, can we hope to gain an overall understanding of "a fully developed morality." These four components are sensitivity, judging, planning, and executing.

Sensitivity Component

The sensitivity component focuses on the ability to recognize—to be aware—that there exists a situation calling forth some level of moral response: being aware of and sensitive to the fact that a moral difficulty does exist and realizing that the welfare of someone is at stake and that one's own actions influence the other's welfare.

A variety of factors have the potential to hinder this component. Among these factors are the ambiguity of the event (one might not realize that a moral issue is at stake), the interpretation of the situation (one might misperceive the situation), and emotional arousal to the occurrence (one could be so emotionally overcome by the event that he or she is unable to respond). According to Rest, to respond morally one must first recognize that a moral response is required. In this regard, Rest views the presence of empathy as a significant factor in sensitizing one to the moral dimension of the situation.

Judging Component

The judging component entails viewing the moral problem in terms of one's own moral ideals and attempting to arrive at some conclusion as to what action is appropriate in terms of one's moral ideals. Whereas the sensitivity component focuses on the realization that a moral concern exists, this component centers on the ideal one envisions as central to the moral concern at hand. In other words, after recognizing that there is a moral concern ("something has happened which violates my moral sense of what is right"), one must be aware of how one's ideals are operative when one encounters a complex moral question. Before Vatican II and the advent of more modern catechetical approaches, this was the component that religious educators stressed. Many readers can recall the admonitions and exhortations that flowed from classroom teachers and religious authorities. Although I have not seen any serious discussion of this issue, it most likely is the case that one reason such warnings and urgings were ineffective was precisely because such pedagogy ignored or was insensitive to other relevant facets of morality. In other words, to stress the judging component at the expense of other components is to short-circuit any serious attempt at helping youth to develop a maturing moral sense. Such a well-intentioned but ill-conceived (and admittedly limited) approach as the exclusive stress on component two does little to advance youth's moral maturity.

Planning Component

At the planning component one actually chooses a course of action that reflects one's valued ideals. Assessing what really can be done in a given situation is also critical for this component. One remains aware of moral ideals, but at the same time one realizes that other dimensions and values are relevant. Situational realities and pressures are given consideration. One seeks a plan of action in accord with personal ideals, yet, at the same time, one recognizes the realities of the situation. Stated another way, even though one might know what one ought to do, one still must choose to do it; this choice is the essence of component three. Psychological studies have pointed out the fact (often known simply by common sense and everyday observation) that an individual's statements as to what he or she will choose to do are often at variance with his or her actual behavior. This discrepancy points to the need to investigate what leads one actually to choose to behave morally.

Executing Component

In the executing component, the person acts on his or her moral decision. This component involves the implementation of one's goals despite various impediments. Consideration is also given to those factors that sustain one's responses over time. The resolution to carry through on one's moral intentions is essential: moral choices alone are not adequate, one must also follow through on one's moral ideals. By focusing on this component, Rest asserts the need not only to view intentions but also the actual behavior.

Rest believes that Kohlberg's moral development theory is best represented by the judging component (component two). Thus, reasoning about justice refers to one's ideals and to what one views as normative; yet it does little in terms of sensitizing one to moral problems or planning how to carry out a moral response, not to mention attempting to sustain the response over time. Moreover, Rest maintains that each component of morality contains both affective and cognitive aspects and that all four components are integral to any full understanding of morality. Finally, each component interacts with other components in the model; thus, Rest's understanding of morality is not linear (as when one component sequentially follows another). Rather, each influences the others. Undue attention to any one component modifies the working of other components. All components are crucial to understanding morality.

I admire Rest's attempt to provide an overall framework for understanding morality (or, more specifically, the moral behavior of an individual in a given situation). At the same time, I would like to add two points to Rest's conceptualization. First, Rest seems to give insufficient attention to developmental features. Such a statement has to be made with caution because Rest is not proposing a developmental model of morality (like Kohlberg does with his developmental theory and stage-development approach). Still, although Rest's sensitivity component takes into account a person's developing capacity to empathize and to be sensitive to his or her surroundings, it is questionable whether this is an adequate discussion of developmental features. In particular I am thinking of the need for a fuller discussion of the identity and intimacy needs that preoccupy the adolescent and young adult and that in turn highly influence youth's understanding of the moral self.

A second caution is also warranted. Rest is writing as a psychologist. He cannot be expected to address the dynamics of mystery that are formulated within the Christian tradition as God's gracious offer of his self-communicating presence. In other words, Christian morality dialogues on another level besides the human. The action of grace (Rom. 8:11) works to transform our very selves into a "wholly new realm of life, one in which the body is completely vivified by the grace of God."[5]

A Christian Perspective of Rest's Model

Our overall approach to Rest's model seeks to translate the insights of psychological science into the faith perspective of the Christian moral tradition. The question can be posed as follows: What features of Christian morality correspond to the four components that Rest considers essential for morality? As the reader might note, in integrating these two dimensions, respect is given to the Catholic theological principle that grace builds on nature. In other words, the model proposed by Rest offers a unique perspective of nature, or how the human comes to experience his or her moral self in everyday decision making. The task is to look more extensively at each of these components in order to discover their Christian features. It is to this task that we now turn.

Sensitivity Component

Sensitivity to moral situations varies among individuals. Recent pronouncements of the American bishops and other religious bodies on nuclear war and on the economy underscore the need for critical awareness and knowledge of complex moral issues. Furthermore, there must exist a sensitivity to the problems and needs of the everyday life situations that confront the Christian. An urgent task for educators is the development of a morality that is situated in the needs of everyday life.

A fruitful way to examine basic human sensitivity is to explore the significance that empathy exercises in the development of morality. Empathy represents a human foundational response for the emergence of Christian behaviors. Empathic experiences orient the person to be aware of the hurt and plight of those in need. Empathy is a naturally occurring phenomenon that orients one to behave altruistically toward others. Accordingly, empathy is the human mechanism that fosters social bondedness and community. This universal experience of empathy blends nicely with Jesus' call for a universal care toward one's brothers and sisters, as in the story of the Good Samaritan. Empathy, moreover, forms the impetus for making real the Gospel's command to love (John 15:17). It is the human capacity to empathize which allows us to feel and to understand the needs, concerns, and cares of another. Furthermore, Jesus' own discipleship vividly portrays this empathic experience. "For we do not have a high priest who is unable to sympathize with our weakness, but one who was tempted in every way that we are, yet never sinned" (Heb. 4:15). Likewise, as the Hebrews writer notes, "he is able to deal patiently with erring sinners, for he himself is beset by weakness" (Heb. 5:2). The writer of Hebrews went to great effort to point out how Jesus is one who experienced our own human suffering. In effect, Jesus' own experiences of human poverty allows him to be a source of care and support for each of us in moments of trial and tribulation. In addition, empathy is a profoundly human experience enabling each Christian to offer his or her gifts to build up the Christian community. Paul's struggles with the Corinthian community point to the empathic experience that underscore any attempt at community building. Gifts given in the Lord (I Cor. 12) are to be used to bring about unity in the Corinthian community. Likewise, in the dispute over speaking in tongues and the dissension caused by eating the food of idols, Paul speaks eloquently of the need to nurture behaviors and gifts that "build up" and bring unity to the community. Awareness of such behaviors is best reflected in an empathic sensitivity toward one's brothers and sisters that is nourished and sustained in a faith community of believers. These very concrete and human experiences of the early church's community building demonstrate the critical importance of an empathic sense. Without this experience of empathy, which provides the human foundation for Paul's appeal, the urging for unity among the Corinthians would be futile.

Judging Component

The judging component, as noted above, refers to the ideals of the faith community. From a Christian perspective, numerous factors deserve consideration. For one, the traditions of the faith community must be ideals to which one can appeal. Aspects of this tradition include the history of the faith community, the authority given the faith community in the Spirit, and the life themes that have nourished the community (for example, the Exodus in the Old Testament and the challenge of conversion in the New Testament). The Christian can also appeal to the ideals of the Christian story which are experienced in the living of discipleship. We have already mentioned that the sources for these ideals, such as the Decalogue and the Sermon on the Mount, are pivotal reference points for the Christian.

Planning Component

Having identified the many ideals involved in a given situation, one must choose an ideal in light of the numerous factors involved in the situation. The decision to endorse a particular plan of action involves the existential reality of a situation as well as pastoral sensitivity. Christian ideals are lived out through the actions and experiences of human beings whose lives always fall short of the Gospel's command to love. Of particular importance for the Christian is the virtue of prudence, which in a broad sense, involves a clarity of purpose and a vision of what is truly possible. Another critical dimension of this component is the need for some "level of value" in order to discern which ideals will be embraced when there are conflicting or competing values. In other words, discernment in Christian life often involves the need to sort out responses in the midst of two competing goods and choose the better, or between two evils and choose the lesser. A good example of this is the case of the public official with limited budgetary resources who must make critical decisions among competing interests, all of which might be worthy and in need of the highest funding possible. In such circumstances it is naturally important that the official have not only clear information regarding the needs of the community but also a clear idea of the ideals that motivate his or her own value choice. Furthermore, any decision to act in a particular way must accept the reality of human suffering as part of one's life (Rom. 5:3–5). Thus, the Christian's decision must not be an attempt to avoid the suffering inherent in the losing of self, the heart of Jesus' message (Matt. 16:24–25).

Executing Component

It is noteworthy that Rest cites Saint Paul when discussing this component. Paul bemoans the fact that "the good that I would, I do not; but the evil which I would not, that I do" (Rom. 7:19). Clearly, intentions are not enough. A firm character, resolute goals, and perseverance are necessary to a moral course of action. For the Christian, this component includes Paul's central focus on the community. The importance of community underscores its pivotal role in the Christian's life. Community sustains the Christian who commits his or her life to virtuous living, the cultivation of habits oriented toward living out the Spirit's fruits (Gal. 5:22).

The Adolescent Experience

Thus far this chapter has shown that an overall conceptual understanding of morality is possible with Rest's criteria. In a similar vein, Christian understandings of morality can give substance to such an overall approach. A key question, however, is how such a framework is integrated with youth's experience. More precisely, one of the most important aspects of any model for morality is how it aids the formation of young people within the faith community.

In a recently published book called *Being Adolescent*, social researchers Mihaly Csikszentmihalyi and Reed Larson document the everyday lives of adolescents. Their findings paint a picture of youth who are moody, restless, and often alienated from the interests and demands of the adult world. What adolescents desire is activity and peer companionship. Their inner selves are often unmotivated; they are subject to frequent periods of inattention that burden their attempts to integrate the demands of maturity.

The book confirms several popular impressions of youth. First, relational concerns are of paramount importance to the adolescent. Second, adolescents often fear periods of solitude and the experience of loneliness. Third, young people are notoriously inefficent in analyzing their life experience and profiting from it. Fourth, adolescents are often unable to articulate their values and goals. "The problem is that adolescents often have no meaningful goals. They have not had the time to attach themselves to anything they consider worthwhile."[6]

Integrating Theory and Practice

As we have seen, the adolescent years pose challenges for religious educators and youth ministers. Integrating Rest's four components, the Christian features of his model and the experiences of adolescents, several instructive pastoral strategies emerge.

Sensitivity Component

Sensitizing adolescents to moral problems and the concerns of others must be a priority for religious educators. Fortunately, the most advanced form of empathy emerges during the adolescent years. With the advent of higher cognitive thinking (formal thought) the adolescent is able to abstract and thus comprehend and empathize with the experiences not only of family and peers (people he or she personally knows) but also of wider social groups (such as other races, the disadvantaged) and individuals with whom he or she had had no contact (such as the starving of Africa). It is important for religious educators to explore with adolescents their understanding of moral problems as well as their feelings toward various moral dilemmas they encounter. Time spent on role playing offers an optimum opportunity for adolescents to become sensitized to the concerns and hurts of others. In such experiences, adolescents personally experience the suffering of others and often gain insight into the other's situation.

Another aspect of this component is the focusing on immediate experience and short-term goals. One common problem when working with adolescents is their difficulty in comprehending long-range consequences for their actions. For example, issues of drug abuse are more likely to be understood by the adolescent when framed in a context of immediate consequences (such as drug use ruins physical health and popularity with peers, or might distract from studies thereby endangering acceptance into college). The advantage of this focus is that it encourages the adolescent to be more attentive.

Finally, adolescents need to be exposed to ways of perceiving values in everyday life situations. Self-inquiry techniques that orient the adolescent to reflect on his or her actions need to be actively encouraged: for example, the adolescent can rank order everything he or she did the preceding day according to some value and say why the rankings were given to particular events. Reflective questions such as "Why do you value those things so highly?" and "What might this tell you about yourself?" are useful. Such reflection helps sensitize the adolescent to "why" he or she is inclined to cherish certain values.

Judging Component

Because relational concerns preoccupy so much of the adolescent's life, questions regarding the adolescent's experience of Jesus are often best viewed in personal terms that adopt a low Christological approach; that is, without ignoring the divinity of Jesus Christ, one places a major emphasis on the humanity of Jesus—his concerns, struggles, and significant experiences. In a similar vein, personal encounter with Jesus in Scripture is decidedly personal and focuses for the adolescent the role he or she exercises in relationship to Jesus Christ (Mark 10:21, where the call to "come follow me" is offered to the rich young man—who most likely is an adolescent— is an excellent example).

Adolescents need a healthy exploration of their own values and a helpful theme for exploring values is unraveling the meaning of commitment. Time is needed to explore with adolescents what in fact they desire to be committed to and how their behaviors reflect these commitments. Commitments allow the adolescent to feel psychically the experience of self-permanency. The numerous changes taking place during the second decade of life leaves many adolescents feeling adrift and unable to find, subjectively, experiences that ratify the values they have been taught. In short, adolescents need to explore the values that represent for them their ideals and which provide them with personal meaning.

Thus, adolescents have few felt experiences of value commitments; they experience their world as aimless and often are without

41

goals. I define the integration of consciously held values and stable, ongoing felt attachments as morally felt foundations (more will be said about this in the next chapter). The development of these foundations in youth deserves the highest priority. Adults must be willing to speak with adolescents of their own value commitments (whether they be relationships, vocational choices, or personal interests); these adult articulations affirm for the adolescent the fact that valued commitments are indeed possible and integral to Christian life.

Planning Component

The task of adolescence is not only to form self-identity through the question, Who am I? but also to give substance to that self-identity by answering the question, What am I about? It is this self-identity that becomes the instrument for value choice. (We will treat this component more fully in the next chapter.)

Once the adolescent's attention has been focused on a moral problem or issue and the ideals or lived values that are central to this experience, he or she must choose what ideal is most operative and consistent with his or her own self-identity. Choosing values becomes especially problematic when discussing issues of social morality (the application of social justice principles to political and international issues). So often social morality involves a complex interplay of issues that do not translate easily into clear decisions: for example, the public official mentioned previously who has a limited amount of money to spend on numerous important projects and must, inevitably, make some hard choices. Likewise, adolescents who must decide whether a dual minimum wage is right or wrong can find positions on both sides of the issue. With these examples, Christians can debate as to what is the proper Christian response, and it would be hard to claim that there is only one Christian position. In various moral dilemmas and personal life issues which adolescents encounter, adults need to help them clarify the various values involved as well as the alternative courses of action possible (with their corresponding values).

Furthermore, due to the idealism of many adolescents, it is important to spend time examining the realities and need for compromise and the limited nature of their efforts, no matter how well-intentioned. Untested by the ambiguities and complexities of the adult world, many adolescents will formulate abstract and unrealistic plans which, when discovered to be unworkable, lead to disillusionment or loss of interest and goals. A classic example of this scenario is the adolescent who ends a retreat resolved to behave in certain ways and champion certain causes. Such idealism is soon held accountable to the realities of immovable structures, the attitudes of uncooperative peers and adults, and the innumerable distractions that inundate the adolescent's life.

Moreover, adolescents are prone to engage in distorted cognitions and faulty belief systems regarding their own selves and perceptions of the world. That is, they often engage in all-or-nothing thinking ("It has to be this way, or else . . . ") and externalization (the idea that something external to the self is the sole cause) or self-deprecating ideas ("I just *have* to do it this way or . . . "). Such thinking leads to much emotional turmoil, distraction, and the inefficient use of psychic energy often exhibited through needless worry or the desire to avoid being alone. Adults can gently challenge adolescents to explore the underlying beliefs and encourage them to accept the realities of their own limits as well as the true meaning of events and situations.

Finally, adolescents need help in coming to terms with influences that dominate their lives. Quite often they are unable to examine reflectively the sources that sway them. More precisely, they need to explore the influence of their peer group and their own capacity to withstand peer pressure. Insight-oriented questions that address the values they see in their peer relationships as well as how they might differ from their peers are helpful. Since peers have a marked influence on the adolescent's behavior, the values and behaviors associated with the adolescent's peers can be a source of real insight and moral growth. In a similar vein, attention needs to be given to larger cultural influences. Quite often the young person is simply unaware that television, advertising, and other cultural factors can be sources of stereotypic attitudes, sexism, and overly materialistic aspirations. Adolescents need the aid of adults in order to examine critically various cultural influences.

Executing Component

Psychologists use the term *self-efficacy* to define the feeling that one possesses the capacity to accomplish one's goals. One of the most crucial tasks in adolescence is the achievement of a sense of self-competence; that is, a confidence that one can bring about a reasonable measure of success in accomplishing one's goals. Without this positive feeling, adolescents are prone to exhibit acutely felt insecurity and retreat from growthful and caring responses; or they might respond in dependent and clinging ways and attempt to find their identity through overidentifying with peers or significant others, thereby limiting their capability for healthy autonomous functioning. Thus, a primary goal for adults ministering to adolescents is to help them reflect on their gifts and talents and on how these qualities are used to build up the community. Youth need, likewise, the experience of a community wherein they can discuss and ask the serious questions that engage them. Without the experience of a supportive community, adolescents can not be expected to accept the challenges of moral commitment. Furthermore, such communal experiences (youth groups, retreats) must honestly face relevant moral issues and problems which adolescents deem significant in their everyday lives.

An underlying theme of Christian faith is the need for nourishment (community, the Eucharist, and so on). Adolescent self-absorbtion needs to be confronted and young people made aware as to how they find sustenance and support if they are not inclined to accept the community's invitation to worship. It is well documented that many adolescents and young adults experience a "time out" period during these developmental years. In other words, for many youth, these years are marked by the absence of any consistent practice of traditional forms of worship. Even so, adolescents are held responsible for seeking deepening understandings of their own behavior. As such, adolescents need input and challenge from adults as to the why of their own behaviors and continual encouragement to seek further self-insight.

The Psychological Environment for the Adolescent's Moral Development

In chapter 1 we noted that multiple dimensions of morality must be addressed in order to provide an optimum framework for assisting the adolescent along the path to moral maturity. In particular, attention was given to the context of moral growth as it pertains to the adolescent's developmental experience as well as specific environmental features which foster this growth throughout the adolescent period. In this regard, two focuses are helpful for the adult minister of youth: first, the family of the adolescent and, second, the role that a valued adult exercises in influencing the moral life of the adolescent.

Family

In the years that I have worked with adolescents in pastoral and clinical settings I have never failed to be struck by the extent to which the family nourishes or limits the adolescent's moral growth. In an age of ongoing stress, economic pressures, dual-career couples, and family dissolutions, the task of moral education in the home becomes particularly challenging.

Though admittedly in many ways subjective, I would like to offer my own pastoral-clinical impressions of what family characteristics are necessary for healthy adolescent moral growth to take place. Over the years I have found recurrent themes and characteristics in what we might term "morally growthful" families. I do not say that all of these characteristics have to be present for the adolescent's moral growth or that any one or two characteristics are more important than others. Nonetheless, my view is that many of these characteristics are highly correlated and that the presence of some often signifies the presence of others.

(A brief discussion of each characteristic follows. After each discussion, a series of questions is offered that may be useful to the adult who ministers to youth.)

Clear norm setting: The adolescent's developmental needs require the clear enunciation of rules and expectations. There are basic psychological reasons for this requirement. First, during adolescence one becomes increasingly aware of his or her impulses. This being the case, there is need for some type of safe environment that provides a sense of felt security from these urges, which at times can seem overwhelming. Parents must never forget that behind the protestations and testing that are part of the adolescent experience there often exists a cry for rules and regulations. In fact, acting out can at times be the young person's veiled plea to the adult to establish rules and provide security. Naturally, the adoles-

45

cent does not realize his or her troublesome behavior reflects this underlying reason, yet it is the sensitive parent who can understand the adolescent rebellion as not only a time when the young person states, "let me be myself," but also, "help me to be myself by giving me guidelines." Such limit setting is not something magically started in the adolescent phase of the child's development (if so, it is a perfect setup for failure). Rather, successful limit setting is the product of lifelong habits of providing guidance in helping the child develop the inner resources necessary for continuing moral growth.

A second reason why norms are necessary is the adolescent experience of change. Adolescence, particularly early and middle adolescence (when troublesome behavior is apt to be most pronounced), is a time of fluid and constant change along a variety of fronts: physical, emotional, social, and intellectual. In the midst of this ongoing change, the young person requires some areas of life that are felt senses of security. Reasonable rules and regulations provide this sense of security.

Adolescent/family focus: Does this adolescent "know" what is expected of him or her? How does this adolescent react to rules? In what ways does this adolescent "test" rules and limit setting? Is the adolescent capable of understanding the reasons for rules?

Giving the reason why: In a family dedicated to moral growth, rules are not just given, they are explained. To set rules without explanation is to create a hollow shell of false security. With time, most adolescents will challenge such a veneer. In addition, the normal storms and stresses of adolescence will easily lead the adolescent to shed such false trappings. A way to view this importance of *why* is to examine the distinction between *authoritarian* and *authoritative*. The former is marked by a rigidity of rules and regulations: the rule is most important. The latter is marked by firmness, fairness, and willingness to explain. Adolescents will naturally rebel against the first, yet the overwhelming number of youth will be appreciative of the second. In addition, adolescents need to feel a sense of respect as they consciously experience their evolving sense of maturing identity. Their newfound intellectual growth as well as the evolving social identities and the acquisition of responsible roles requires parents to "listen" to their adolescents' opinions as well as share with them the reasons for imposing limits.

46

Adolescent/family focus: Do family rules and regulations show a basic and proper respect for who the adolescent is and what he or she is becoming? Does the adolescent know why certain rules exist within the family? Does the family provide the opportunity for the adolescent to offer input on rules?

Feelings toward rules: It is not enough that limits be expressed within the family. What is also needed is a sense of loyalty and appreciation of family rules. If parents simply dictate rules, then these rules can easily take on a sterile quality. Adolescents need to know that rules are accepted within the family because they are valued and respected. There can exist a deep reverence or even a sense of playfulness about a rule. The reason that an affection for rules is critical is that consistent moral behavior rarely results merely from attitudes or beliefs. Emotions energize rules; they provide a bonding and trust that sustains fidelity toward the value which, ideally, forms the basis for the rule. Furthermore, a family that invests in rules in an emotionally healthy way exhibits a far greater level of communication since what is apparent is a more significant investment of each family member's self. An adolescent is well aware of the underlying emotional tone within the family. For example, in a family where the privacy of each member is respected, enunciating how members treat one another will not simply be a proscription or a guideline. On the contrary, there exists a deep respect for each family member and such a norm is stated with a deep sense of urgency for all in the family. One gets the impression that in such families a clear understanding of solitude and intimacy is respected. Violations of such rules, likewise, are met with clear disapproval. Because a morally healthy family feels so deeply about certain rules, they do not allow violations to occur unnoticed. At the same time, attention needs to be given to the fact that family rules can mirror unhealthy emotional responses. A classic example of this is the parent who, because of unwarranted fear, places on the adolescent unreasonable restrictions which lead the young person to limit his or her normal self-discovery. Limit setting at times masks unhealthy parental responses, such as dependency, fear, and guilt.

Adolescent/family focus: Do parents and children have feelings about the rules that govern family members' behavior? Do parental actions show an overinvolvement in rule setting? Do parents overreact when rules are violated? Do adolescents react appropriately to rules? Is there overreaction on the adolescent's part?

Admitting mistakes: Families that are growing morally together are families where perfect behavior is not expected. In such families both parents and children have permission to admit that all is not always well. This is one dimension that, when lacking, becomes a foundation for crippling guilt, low self-esteem, and inevitable failure. Families where forgiveness is not encouraged foster unrealistic expectations and chronic senses of inadequacy for family members. Often such families claim that mistakes are understood, while in reality there exists a tacit assumption that certain behaviors are always expected and when transgressions occur, they point to the family member's inadequacy. As a clinician, one behavior that I always look for in parents is their ability to "apologize" to their children, and to feel comfortable with their own limits and imperfections. The adult's ability to admit mistakes is crucially important for the moral development of the child.

In homes where acknowledgment of mistakes is not experienced by children, they may develop the erroneous notion that to be an adult is to be perfect, along with standards of perfection that no child can possibly live up to. To state this in a more positive way: An adult who is comfortable with his or her own limits and can admit his or her mistakes becomes a particularly significant presence in the child's life. Such a child grows to understand, in a safe and secure way, the experience of human failing and, more importantly, becomes comfortable with an inescapable fact of life, one with which every adolescent will need to come to terms.

Acknowledging a mistake is an important way for adults to demonstrate respect for the adolescent and build self-esteem, two qualities which are essential for the development of moral growth. When we offer an apology we say to another that we value him or her so much that we want to acknowledge in our relationship with them all that is discrepant in our desired way of being-in-the-relationship. Their presence in our lives is so significant, in other words, that we will not tolerate any misunderstandings or less than adequate behaviors. At times, this acknowledgment of transgressions and the showing of respect can take place in small yet potentially enriching ways. I periodically teach a workshop to Jesuit seminarians who are about to begin their regency (this is a two- or three-year period of teaching before the Jesuit begins his theology studies leading to ordination). I repeatedly share with these men the importance of fostering self-respect in youth and note that a profound way to do this is by admitting one's own mistakes. For example, a teacher clearly expects that students will arrive on time to class and that if they are late they will have an explanation or written excuse. Yet, it is important to ask whether we live by the same standards that we demand of the adolescents we teach. A teacher might periodically be late because of a meeting or some other valid reason. In such cases the teacher should also take thirty seconds and in a natural and matter of fact way explain to the class why he or she is late. This need not be a long or elaborate explanation, but it does need to be explained. Such behaviors are tremendously important for communicating to adolescents a sense of personal self-worth. These actions show that adults respect adolescents and value them for who they are.

Adolescent/family focus: How comfortable is this family with acknowledging their limitations? How easily can they admit mistakes to one another? Does the adolescent feel under pressure? Does he or she believe "I must be perfect?" What is the quality of the communication in the home when discussing limits and imperfections. Is there a sense in the family that "we can learn from one another"?

Ambiguity: A family committed to moral growth must not only set up rules, the family must also learn to be comfortable with a sense of ambiguity. A consistent learning experience that families must confront when they have adolescents is youth's tendency to "test the limits." The adolescent will involve himself or herself in behaviors that force the adult to set up new rules. More importantly, this "testing" can prove to be a fruitful opportunity for the entire family to grow morally. For example, a middle adolescent who challenges the family's practice of attending Sunday services forces the entire family to examine the reasons why they attend religious services. Of course parents can simply state rules and insist that they be followed. However, such simplistic thinking denies the whole family the opportunity to reflect on previously sacrosanct beliefs and to struggle with more authentic reasons for some behaviors. At times the adolescent's behavior can challenge or even deny the family's most basic beliefs, such as the belief in God. Another example of this might be an adolescent's involvement in a sexual relationship. How is the family to respond to this situation? Such questions confront essential belief systems and force a deeper exploration of values and behavior. Being able to deal honestly and creatively with many situations can help parents come to a better understanding of their own values and can lead to more open and honest communication. For example, if there is a policy at home that prohibits adolescent drinking under any circumstances, how do parents respond when the adolescent states that he will be at a graduation party supervised by other parents at a friend's home? What do the parents say to the college undergraduate who comes home from college and desires to drink on a few occasions? There are no simple answers to such questions. On the other hand, a promising quality in morally healthy families is the desire to dialogue and share views and feelings on such topics. Without abdicating their authority, parents must be willing to examine the ambiguity of numerous situations that confront them when there are adolescent children in the home. This dialogue enables all in the family to reflect more deeply on their values

Adolescent/family focus: How comfortable is the family with discussing various rules? How does the family cope with moral questions and working out solutions?

Keep on growing: Another dimension of the family that exhibits moral health is the desire to keep on growing in their understanding of their values. A way to view this dimension is to view a family as a group who are committed to inquiry. This means that they desire to look continually at the sources and reasons for their moral values. In such families there is a healthy sense of asking the question, Why? This *why* is not a way to attack parental values. Rather, it is a legitimate search always to give the most significant meaning and authentic expression to the values the family holds.

For such a dimension to exist within the family, there must be a high degree of communication. An example of this inquiry is the discussion of issues related to social justice. An adolescent might, for example, formulate moral judgments on political and social events that are at variance with the traditional beliefs of the parents. In the morally healthy (and growing) family, there can be a free, even spirited discussion of various reasons for holding certain political views. An underlying principle of this dimension is the parents' ability to not only "listen" to their children, but, indeed, to learn from them. Although surprising, this principle makes sense from a psychological viewpoint: only when one feels secure and committed in a healthy way to his or her view can one truly take the stance that learning is possible from others. In pastoral-clinical situations I often ask the parent(s), "What have you learned from your adolescent this week?" or (and perhaps a little less threatening) "What have you learned about yourself from living with this adolescent in your home?" Such questions can serve as a catalyst for later thoughtful examination by the adult.

Adolescent/family focus: How open is this family? Are family discussions open to new ideas? Can reasons be given for beliefs that the family holds? Is there a sense in this family that members really do value learning from one another?

Taking responsibility: An essential dimension of moral growth in any family is acceptance among family members of personal responsibility. That is, every member of the family has knowledge of what is expected of him or her. Furthermore, when mistakes or errors are made, the individual family member is capable of acknowledging the error. Another ingredient of this dimension is the ability to accept consequences of actions. This acceptance is vital, indeed critical, for moral growth. Healthy adolescent development is impossible unless parents are committed to addressing the children's need to take personal responsibility for their behavior. A corollary to this responsibility is the parents' capacity to be consistent in behavior. When parental consistency is lacking, adolescents are not pushed to examine and reflect on their behaviors. In other words, if a behavior is punished on one occasion and disregarded on another, the adolescent is more likely to focus on "how" to avoid punishment rather than reflect on the "why" of behavior.

Adolescent/family focus: Does the adolescent know what is expected of him or her? Is there consistency in parental behavior?

Stress the positive: A family that is growing morally focuses on positive behavior rather than negative consequences. Living a moral life is not simply the result of obeying rules or experiencing punishment. Rather, the moral life arises from emphasis on helping others and showing care. This statement might appear obvious to some. Yet, it is surprising how many families equate morality with prohibitions and regulations rather than positive, growthful caring that emphasizes the needs and hurts of others.

Adolescent/family focus: What is the quality of care in this family? What is the level of sensitivity in this family? How does the family show care to others outside the family? Is this care shown not only as individuals but also as a family group?

Having outlined the dimensions of the family that is growing morally, we now turn to a brief description of various "types" of families.

The morally conversant family: The atmosphere and dynamics that are experienced in this family are the dimensions noted above. Limit setting and the understanding of consequences are known by all family members. In addition, family members place high priority on communicating their views to one another. These families are willing to discuss issues and explore together underlying values. A primary theme these families experience is a respect for various views of family members and a willingness to confront together the various questions and issues which arise in the family. Finally, these families are outer focused: they provide adequate attention to each one's needs and yet give balanced priority to activities that address the needs and hurts of those outside the family. Such families are involved with other people's lives rather than overly preoccupied with their own concerns.

The committed family: These families are quite similar to the morally conversant families noted above. However, in these families what is often lacking is the desire or ability to confront the new or unforeseen. In most respects, these families show a high degree of sensitivity toward one another and value limit setting and responsibility (by responsibility we refer to the adolescent's owning of his or her decisions and being held accountable for them). However, these families are usually not as open to broad discussion of moral issues as are morally conversant families nor are they as willing to explore the ambiguous and new situations that are often part of the adolescent experience of family. Confronting ambiguity is potentially disruptive for these family members.

The rigid family: In this family the main focus is on the acceptance of parental authority and the obeying of rules. What is valued in this family is the rule. Explanations of rules and asking why are not encouraged. A prominent feature of these families is adolescent rebellion as the young person seeks to establish an identity separate from the family experience.

The dependent family: This family is very much like the rigid family above. The essential difference is the instrumental nature of the rules that exist within the family. In other words, rules are not obeyed for rules' sake (as in the rigid family). Rather, rules are obeyed because they provide the parent with a means for perpetuating the dependency of the adolescent on the parent. In such families there is often an intrusive nature to the parents' behavior. The adolescent is often lacking privacy or a sense of individuality. In these homes, great pressure is placed on the adolescent to conform to parental expectations and model himself or herself after the parent.

The Laissez-faire family: Unlike the rigid family that emphasizes obedience to rules, the laissez-faire family is noted for its absence of rules. In such families adolescents are often allowed to engage in a wide variety of behaviors without challenge. Unfortunately, such parental neglect will lead the adolescent to engage in disruptive, even harmful behavior in order to gain attention from the parents and to force adult response to the adolescent's provocative behavior.

The Role of the Valued Adult in the Adolescent's Moral Life

We have already noted the need for adolescent separation from parental authority. Indeed, such venturing out from parental authority is critical for adolescent moral growth. The transition from exclusive reliance on parental authority to a responsible young adulthood (wherein the late adolescent takes personal responsibility for his moral life while being open to the advice and counsel of others) is eased considerably by the adolescent's alliance with other valued adults. Such adult figures in the adolescent's life provide several functions. First, these adults (whether teacher, coach, relative, boss, or someone else) provide a source of encouragement and support. These relationships serve as a source for moral guidance when parental influence is waning. Second, other adults furnish a necessary foundation that supports the adolescent's belief in the essential value of his or her moral self. Because of the need for parental separation, adolescents are often unable to turn to parents as moral reference points. This inability arises from the fact that to follow parental demands rekindles feelings of the dependency from which the adolescent is desperately trying to escape. The adult serves as a viable alternative who can communicate the same ideals, but in a way that is less threatening. This fact points out the mistake that some adults make when they try to be "like" adolescents. Young people do not need "relevant" adults; they need caring adults whose own lives are a witness to the values that they struggle to understand. Third, other adults furnish the adolescent with an alternative source of moral guidance that encourages exploration and deepening inquiry. The adult's presence encourages an exploration of values without the threat of rejection, which is an ever-present felt threat in the parent-adolescent dialogue. At the same time, the adult can provide the necessary structure that allows for a searching that is responsible and growthful for the adolescent.

The dynamics of the adult-adolescent relationship (as opposed to the parent-adolescent relationship) needs some exploration. In other words, what psychological experience is allowing for this bond to evolve between a high school or college youth and a trusted adult? The psychological construct described as the ego ideal acts as the glue that fashions and solidifies the adult-adolescent relationship. This vital psychological mechanism is critical to our appreciation of the adolescent's struggle to fashion and accommodate an evolving moral self.

The ego ideal has received sparse attention in psychological literature. In discussion centering on the internal psychological dynamics of moral growth, attention has usually focused on the superego. "The concept of the ego ideal has played of late a rather insignificant role in the psychology of adolescence."[7]

Historically, the ego ideal has often been confused with the superego. The apparent reason for this confusion is the dual nature Freud saw in the development of a person's moral orientation. That is, according to Freud, there exist two features necessary for the psychological development of personal morals: idealization and prohibition. A close reading of Freud's writing shows that various interpretations were given to the terms *superego* and *ego ideal*. Eventually, however, Freud's final position on the source of intrapsychic morality was the incorporation of the ego ideal into the superego with the latter being the dominant psychological structure.[8]

More recent psychological accounts have focused on separating the concept of "ego ideal" from "superego" and pointing to the ego ideal's unique characteristics as a source for moral growth during the adolescent period. Essentially, the function of the ego ideal is related to wish fulfillment or the attainment of some desired state. Whereas the superego's function resides in self-criticism and prohibition, the ego ideal represents the self's wish to obtain a desired state. As the psychoanalyst Peter Blos notes, "the superego is an agency of prohibition, while the ego ideal is an agency of aspiration."[9]

The ego ideal's significance in the adolescent years resides in its pivotal role in fostering the adolescent's separation from parents. In the early adolescent years the young person must work through a period of rather volatile feelings toward the parents. In addition, the adolescent becomes disillusioned by his or her growing realization of parental inadequacies. Whereas in childhood the child uncritically accepts parental behaviors and rules, the adolescent, responding to growing critical awareness and the need to loosen parental ties, is apt to respond critically and in a pointed fashion to parental shortcomings. The adolescent, troubled by the waning of parental ties, seeks refuge in an omnipotent self, fads and cursory interests, or group ideals in order to assuage a felt inner void. That is, the adolescent seeks what we might term a psychological source of support to fill the disillusionment often arising from the troubled realization of an ambivalence toward parents.

Fortunately, as adolescence proceeds, the young person is able to shed his or her self-absorbed ways and peripheral distractions and gradually adopt personal values that are both functional and adaptable in the adult world, and which in turn reflect growing moral maturity. The ego ideal shifts from being a source of self-focus (used to create idealistic strivings) or peer attachment (highly focused and often emotionally charged relationship with the other in which the attraction for the other is fed by the ego ideal) and becomes, as a consequence, a repository for appropriate cultural values and a growing moral stance that allows the maturing adolescent to adapt to the world. The esteemed adult serves as a crystallization of what the ego ideal might become (what the adolescent desires to be). The trusted adult provides a supportive presence wherein the adolescent's striving for ideals and moral maturity receives grounding and the hope of fulfillment. At the same time, the knowledgeable adult offers a healthy moderating influence that prevents the adolescent's ego ideal from fueling unrealistic, unobtainable, and often tyrannical aspirations. An example of this latter point is the late adolescent who is never satisfied and is overly critical of any attempt for a solution to a problem or difficulty in a relationship. In this instance, unrealistic expectations render the adolescent subject to an almost perpetual unhappiness inasmuch as he or she is never able to accommodate the ego ideal's unrealistic strivings. Still, if we simply view the internal psychological dynamics of the ego ideal, then we lose the richness of the ego ideal as a source for interpersonal and social interaction. It is this social nature of the ego ideal that reflects the value constellation which crystallizes during the adolescent period into a maturing moral system for adulthood.

The ego ideal is bonded with a moral stance. In essence, a mature ego ideal (which is well on its way by the later adolescent years) is nourished through a gradual identification with a growing sense of personal values that leads to an increasing sense of autonomy. In the adolescent years what transpires in normal development is the shedding of idealized parental standards and the adoption of an increasingly personalized value system. The final stage of ego ideal formation occurs in late adolescence when the adolescent, with greater ease than in the earlier adolescent years, integrates parental and other adult expectations and standards with his or her own moral views to arrive at a meaningful and coherent value system. The ego ideal emerges as a source for values whereby the adolescent gradually identifies with a personalized value orientation that in turn provides a greater adaptive capacity for the adult world. In the course of normal development and implicit in this value identification is the presence of societal norms and the significance accorded some acceptable level of prosociality and caring. (Hopefully, too, the ego ideal reflects not only societal norms but ideals that offer a standard for what society might be—an ideal of justice, for example.)

The ego ideal represents a unique psychic structure for value because of its aspirational drive to become something beyond the present. In essence, the ego ideal represents a striving for something yet to be realized. The ego ideal possesses an aspirational quality that seeks to achieve the self's ideals. Blos hints at this feature when he notes the ego ideal is an "agency of aspiration."

I experienced a situation while teaching secondary school that points out the aspirational quality of values. Jim, a high school junior, was periodically difficult during class. He displayed attention-seeking behaviors and showed a strong need for adult approval. Jim came from a difficult home background. His father was an alcoholic and his mother was a dominating figure in his life. One day a classmate, John, was disrupting class. As the teacher I corrected John and requested he stay and see me after class. At the end of the class period John came to me quite upset. He accused me of not being fair. He stated I allowed Jim to get by with actions that I would not allow from him. He pointed out that I displayed a more tolerant attitude toward Jim. In effect, John was demanding that I be fair in my classroom discipline. As the teacher I was well aware of this discrepancy (although it was most certainly overdramatized by John). I explained to John that as the teacher in the class it was important to be fair with students. At the same time, I explained that as a teacher I also strived to understand my students and desired to know why they acted as they did in the classroom. I simply asked John to reflect on whether he and Jim were the same as people. Thus, in this particular situation, I was attempting to go beyond fairness. I was encouraging John to aspire to a value that incorporated compassion and sensitivity. I was challenging him to aspire to be something more. Of course such an approach would not work if there was not an essential level of empathy and compassion in John. From a psychological perspective, I was directly appealing to a developing ego ideal that was gradually incorporating an authentic and personally meaningful value system.

The reader perhaps can glimpse the relevancy of the ego ideal to the adult-adolescent relationship. As the adolescent in high school and college sheds parental ties and grows increasingly distrustful of the adult world, he or she is led to invest psychically in an overly self-focused way, or in peers or some cause, thereby providing an object for his or her idealizations. Consequently, there is a need to provide the adolescent with alternative models to which he or she can psychically attach. Adult role models become alternative ego-ideal objects to which the adolescent can bond as he or she slowly incorporates this ideal of the adult into his or her own growing ego ideal. In effect, the trusted adult is a bridge for the adolescent's growing aspiration to become a moral person. The adult, by his or her attitude, behavior, and manner, gives "substance" to the adolescent's developing aspiration and the adult's presence says to the adolescent that, yes, such ideals are obtainable. A fondness for a teacher or coach in the secondary school years provides the adolescent with a tremendous relief. A college professor or sensitive campus minister likewise occupies a pivotal role for the adolescent who is more sharply constructing his or her personal value system. One of the most significant needs of education and ministry today is that they provide students with teachers and other personnel who are committed to professed value systems and who are present to students both in and out of the classroom thereby offering youth the needed attachment so pivotal for moral growth.

CHAPTER THREE

Conscience and
the Adolescent Moral Self

In order to examine the adolescent's moral self, we must explore the role of conscience in the moral life. We will begin with a short look at the Christian notion of conscience. Next we will examine the development of conscience. Finally we will set forth the dynamics of conscience with particular attention to conscience's functioning in the adolescent years.

A Christian View of Conscience

The Christian notion of conscience can most easily be expressed as the moral quality essential for being human. It originates in the depth of the self and is experienced as the call to respond lovingly in the concrete, existential situation of one's life. In effect, conscience is the *invitation* to respond morally. I would like to extend the metaphor of invitation to explore the meaning of conscience. The individual is both the host and the hoped-for guest. Conscience involves making the host aware of the opportunity to make an invitation. In other words, a critical function of conscience is to be a source of *recognition* that a moral issue or dilemma is at stake. "There is something wrong here." "This is a moral issue." At the same time, the desired guest, hopefully, will pause before accepting the invitation. That is, another function of conscience is its *deliberative* nature. There is pause for reflection and thought before acting.

Furthermore, before sending out the invitation the host might consult with others as to whom to invite. Likewise, the invited guest will at times seek the counsel of others as to whether to accept. To extend the metaphor, the host might need to be prompted by others before issuing an invitation. In a similar vein, a guest might need the nudge of others in order to respond. What we are seeking to point out is that another function of conscience is its capacity for *openness*. There is a dimension of conscience that learns from others.

Conscience must not be equated with moral knowledge. Rather, conscience functions as the means to *discern* values in an actual situation, thereby leading one to initiate behaviors that mirror one's core sense of value. Moral knowledge (ethical codes, knowledge of doctrines and moral theories) energize conscience, but conscience is not knowledge. (As a historical aside, this perspective is at variance with the ancient Greek notion of knowledge as virtue, that is, one who knows the Good will do the Good.) This distinction is helpful in underscoring how conscience is distinct from Kohlberg's moral reasoning. One gets the impression in reading Kohlberg that his view is heavily weighted to morality as knowledge. His moral theory emphasizes that if we could just get moral reasoning "right" (use the right reasons, which would place us at a higher stage), then we would do right. Such, unfortunately, is far too often not the case.

Conscience is not the moral law; rather, conscience functions as the means for *interiorizing* the moral law. In this sense, conscience serves as the link for communicating the personal and unique role to which every man and woman is called in salvation history. This link reveals not only one's fundamental response to God's self-communicating presence, it also calls one to an awareness of one's bonding with and responsibility to others. Thus there exists a *social and communal* function for conscience. Interestingly, psychologists are increasingly emphasizing the social and affiliative aspects of human nature and the possibility of an altruistic basis for human behavior. There is a growing consensus among those who study the psychological development of the child that the self has an inherently prosocial nature. Developmentally, this "social capacity" is reflected in increasingly caring and sensitive reactions toward others. Obviously, such a potential requires a supportive environment as well as positive nurturing experiences in order that this caring sensitivity might grow to develop as a welcome ally for one's moral decisions. The point to be made, however, is the significance of this capacity that serves as an essential grounding for the other-centered view of conscience which we propose in this chapter.[1]

Conscience is the guiding light for one's behavior (Rom. 13: 5, 14:23), yet it remains ever fragile. The frailty of conscience results from its intimate tie to self. That is, conscience is not an ethereal concept. Conscience remains the moral source for personhood, residing in the person *as person*. As such, conscience is wedded to the human limitations and personal shortcomings that accompany all growth and development, and the demands and struggles of adolescence burden conscience in numerous ways.

In chapter 1 we examined a variety of developmental issues that must be taken into consideration when discussing adolescent morality, among them the fact that an adolescent can yield his or her responsibility for decisions to the demands of the peer group. This overidentification with peers can sometimes result in foolish, even risky, behaviors that have the potential for disastrous consequences. In such cases, the adolescent finds the pressure from external influences so overwhelming that he or she is unable to resist peer demands. As a consequence, moral decisions are at times decisions of peers rather than a true reflection of the adolescent's inner sense of value. On the other hand, an adolescent can be so introspective and self-critical that he or she fails to consider positive aspects of the self, thereby contributing to a virtual paralysis in decision making or a plague of recurring self-doubt. As a result, the adolescent comes to be motivated more by fear and worry rather than by authentic self-expression. In short, conscience energizes the moral self, yet its susceptibility to influence from developmental needs and its capacity for false conclusions renders it a "fragile reality" that needs constant care and attention.[2]

In the brief explanation given above we come to view a broadened definition of conscience that goes beyond "right and wrong." In essence, we define conscience as the central moral experience of personhood that allows for the ongoing discernment of value in concrete life situations. Moreover, this realization of value is continually broadened. It is radically other-centered, increasingly incorporating an interpersonal sensitivity that is caring and compassionate and places life decisions more and more within the context of the needs of the human community. Conscience viewed as an evolving realization of other-centered value accepts the demands for self-sacrifice and the deepening commitment to ideals which reflect a discerning and loving stance. Viewed this way, conscience is nourished and sustained by the self-communicating presence of grace, yet it answers to the realities of human development. As such, conscience formation takes place within the struggles, joys, and disappointments of human life and its significance unfolds as it is threaded through the developmental needs and decisions arising from human maturation. As we noted, conscience fuels, energizes, and sustains the moral self. In order to gain understanding of the adolescent moral self, we must turn our attention to the nature of the human conscience.[3]

The Psychology of Conscience Development

Before addressing the psychology of conscience, it is helpful to note a current discussion taking place within both Catholic and Protestant circles regarding the possibility of a truely distinctive Christian ethic. For the sake of simplicity, the nature of the debate can be posed in this way: is there an ethic that is distinctively Christian? For example, is there something that a Christian might do that would uniquely differ from the behavior of a Muslim or an agnostic humanist? Does Christian faith lead to behaviors that are unique or distinctive? I believe that every person, given their psychological nature (what I will touch upon shortly as an empathic capacity) and an adequate upbringing (nurturing family life and adequate role models), would engage in behaviors that are honest, caring, and self-sacrificing. At the same time, however, the intention and rationale for engaging in such behavior (the reasons one gives) portray a uniquely Christian ethic. Thus the Christian rationale for loving behavior is rooted in the Christian message of the Gospel, which challenges one to ongoing conversion and the demands of discipleship. Any psychological approach to conscience must be able to provide a basis for not only the everyday caring behaviors that any person can be expected to engage in but also the motivational and reflective aspects of personal intention. The psychology of conscience that we offer fulfills both of these demands. The various dimensions that we will shortly delineate suffice to offer a psychological basis for what might be termed Christian behavior and also provide a psychological foundation for motivation and intention (the former is highlighted through dimensions such as empathy and guilt whereas the latter is provided through dimensions such as idealization and teleology).

In order to address the dynamics of conscience functioning, we must first explore the psychological origins of conscience. Surprisingly, until recently, little attention has been given to understanding a source for conscience that differs in any way from the standard superego formulation. Equally important, there has been little consideration as to how conscience functions in the adolescent years.

The psychology of conscience has its roots in psychoanalytic theory, which in turn originates with Freud and emphasizes psychic drives, instincts, and internal psychological dynamics. Traditionally, psychoanalytic theory viewed the conscience as being incorporated within the superego. The superego is that psychic structure reponsible for self-criticism and censorship as well as the source for personal self-esteem. "Unfortunately, it is not always clear even in Freud's own writing what part of the superego is being talked about when the word is used—the conscious part called conscience, the unconscious self-critical part, or the partly conscious and partly unconscious part that has to do with self-love and self-esteem."[4]

The superego is the source for both prohibition (that which one is forbidden) and idealization (that which one desires to become). The former is termed the conscience whereas the latter is identified as the ego ideal. Given a healthy emotional tie between parent and child, the child comes to repress instinctual urges and introject parental desires and wishes and increasingly identifies with the same sex parent and later with other authority figures. This process of incorporating the values and characteristics of the parent is known as introjection whereas modeling oneself after the valued adult is termed identification. Consequently, over time, the child grows to understand what is expected of him or her through both internalized demands and expectations and the learning accompanying the observation of everyday adult behavior. In psychoanalytic theory, a compromise develops between the demands of the child to possess the parent and the strict cultural norms that forbid such union; this psychic compromise is the formation of the superego. The superego evolves as the resolution of the child's desire. In essence, the child, although he or she cannot possess the parent, can become "like" the parent. The superego serves as the psychic structure for the child's incorporation of the parent to the self. "The internalized parent, or superego, then serves as both a prohibition of instinctual gratification and as a model for idealistic strivings."[5]

It is understandable how many readers might be dissatisfied with moral development as explained by psychoanalytic theory. For one, the theory is heavily biased against the feminine. Early psychoanalytic theorists such as Freud were heavily influenced by their cultural values and mores.[6] In addition, discussing conscience at the age of four to six (the age when the Oedipus complex occurs) leaves unanswered the vital question of the possibility of earlier precursors of morality that are more in line with the fundamentally other-centered value approach of conscience that we have set forth.[7] And lastly, psychoanalytic theory has been heavily criticized for its narrow focus on internal psychological dynamics and the conflictual view it holds of the child-parent bond.

My own view is that one need not endorse every tenet of psychoanalytic theory in order to recognize the importance of the parent-child bond. A helpful aid to distill the insight gathered from the parent-child bond is to view it as an emotionally charged and enduring bond of attachment that has both a biological and psychological basis. In other words, the development of the child's moral self is indeed intimately tied to his or her relationship with primary caretakers, most usually, and at least initially, the mother. The attachment of child is critical to the formation of the child's sense of self. Most certainly, healthy psychic development requires a nurturing and reliable experience. In the process of becoming his or her own person, there must take place a psychological separation from the parents and a felt-sense that one's own selfhood increasingly functions in a more autonomous manner. Having acquired this differentiation from the mother, the child must in turn master a progression of developmental tasks that encourage a sense of self-mastery and emotional experiences of bonding with others that both gratify the child and stimulate further development. In order to accomplish this process the child will incorporate aspects of parental values and identify with parental behaviors. Above all, the likely candidates for intense and enduring attachments are parents and other family members who are experienced by the child as nurturing and reliable resources for his or her own safety and development.

Nonetheless, the superego view of conscience is limiting. Indeed, the case must be made for a separate psychic source for conscience that is independent of the superego. Moreover, this separate source for conscience provides the basis for the broadened definition of conscience we noted at the beginning of this chapter. That is, conscience understood as rooted in the experience of other-centered value.

Recent formulations of the psychoanalytic theory of morality have sought to portray a source for morality that is present well before the emergence of the superego.

More contemporary understandings of moral development have addressed the positive nurturing presence of care givers, particularly the mother, as a source for conscience and early moral development. Additionally, the positive experiences displayed in such a supportive relationship elicit a secure attachment bond that fosters the child's internalization of moral values (dos and don'ts). Further, early child development—even as early as the first few years of life—shows children's readiness to display "early moral emotions." These emotions (hurt feelings, positive feelings of sharing, shame, and so on) point to an inchoative moral sense that is prior to the forming of the superego. Finally, the presence of empathy in the early childhood years indicates an elementary moral self that is fundamentally geared toward care and sensitivity.[8] All in all, the current understanding of the child's early years strongly suggests the emergence of morality well before the traditional forming of superego that is thought to be resolved around the sixth year of life. In turn, this more contemporary understanding provides a psychological basis for conscience as other-centered value; these early forms of conscience's expression confirm our view of the other-centered focus of conscience.

In addition to arguing for conscience as prior to the superego, we can delineate the contrast between conscience and superego in order to highlight the inadequacies of the latter as the source for a healthy moral sense of self.

For one, superego is wedded to finding ways of acceptance; that is, the superego directs one to adopt parental views and attitudes—to love like the parent loves in order that one also finds love (from the parent). The child's dutiful adherence to the internalized parent creates a safe haven in which the child can receive love. Likewise, the superego is inseparably linked to authority and the need for approval. Ironically, when one accedes to the demands of the superego, one is in essence adhering to an external sense of authority (that from which the superego derives its source—the parental commands it has internalized). As a consequence, the superego is, essentially, unable to incorporate an autonomous and maturing moral sense independent of parental influence. In this sense, the superego is wedded to the past rather than a source for autonomy and a maturing moral sense that is capable of making responsible moral decision. Further, this linkage to the past stifles the creative thrust which is so necessary for dealing with future life encounters that are ambiguous and unplanned.

In a similar vein, the values that the superego champions and promotes are rooted in one's life history and the choices of one's past life. These values are in some sense primitive for they use as their reference point the prohibitions and demands of childhood. More important, the reasons for adopting values as integral to one's core experience, the actual "owning" of values (which is primarily a task of the adolescent years) is not possible with the superego. Responsible moral decision making requires personal reflection and the adoption of a personal value system that is consciously articulated and continually evaluated. Unfortunately, the superego is focused not on this essential aspect of maturity but takes shape in prolonged and unreflective guilt responses that in reality are often burdensome. The adult, for example, who feels guilty over an action that is appropriate, is most likely responding to this unrelenting demand of the internalized parent (the superego) and is experiencing the lingering vestiges of parental prohibitions. To be sure, the superego is not simply the source of prohibitions and demands. On the contrary, the superego also internalizes the loving, nurturing, and caring aspects of the parents. Yet, the psychoanalytic tradition, though admitting this fact, has overwhelmingly expressed the superego as forbidding and demanding rather than caring and nurturing. The superego, in essence, is fundamentally an agent of reproachment, criticism, and punishment.

Another limitation of the superego that is of great consequence is the fact that the values cherished by the superego can have an essentially amoral flavor. How can this be so? The reason for this fact lies in the superego's link to culture. The superego is led to uphold cultural norms. The destructive values of parents (which they also internalized from their own cultural upbringing) are internalized by the child. Consequently, if the parents are raised in a racist culture then racist values are not only held by the parents (often in subtle ways) but also internalized by the child. Eli Sagan captures better than anyone the stark limitations forged from the superego's tie to culture:

> The dependence of the superego on the *particular* society in which it exists underlines a fatal flaw in the theory of the superego as representing the *moral* function within the psyche. Far from carrying out the task of morality in the psyche, *the superego is essentially amoral and can be as easily immoral as moral. Within a slave society, the superego legitimates slavery. Within a racist or sexist society, the superego demands racism and sexism. And in a Nazi society, the superego commands one to live up to genocidal ideals.*[9]

It is for this reason that a criminal can be said to have a highly developed superego. That is, within the criminal culture the antisocial personality functions within the ethical code of criminals. Such a person's superego might be well defined, yet devoid of any meaningful sense of other-centered value. In this instance, the criminal dutifully follows the dictates of the superego. However, one can correctly deny that the criminal's actions are moral.

The influence of culture is readily apparent on the formation of the adolescent's superego. Often adolescents can internalize the nurturing ideals of their parents, yet hold onto racist and stereotypic attitudes. More than likely, these attitudes are a reflection of parental and other adult authorities.

It is also important to explore a related feature of the superego's link to culture. Culture not only indirectly influences superego formation through the adolescent's internalization of the parent's cultural values, the culture also has its own direct effect on the adolescent. The resolution of the superego is renegotiated in the adolescent years as the child reworks and builds a new relationship with parents. The prevailing values of the culture impact on the adolescent's superego as the adolescent strives to internalize a coherent sense of internal rules and commands to guide behavior. Within the past few decades we have two excellent examples of this phenomenon. The student unrest of the sixties and early seventies had a direct influence on many adolescents and young adults as they internalized values that often had a countercultural flavor. Likewise, the adolescents and young adults of the eighties have adopted numerous values from what may commentators have branded the narcissism and "me too-ism" of the culture. This uncritical acceptance of the cultural winds has spawned a generation of adolescents who are prone to be self-absorbed and often less interested in social causes and humanitarian concerns than were their counterparts of only a generation before.

Given the superego's ties to the inevitable limitations of cultural value, the importance of conscience is readily apparent. It is the moral force of conscience that overcomes the cultural eclipse that consigns well-intentioned men and women to moral blindness. People who strive to live good lives are all too often unaware of the stereotypic and degrading views they hold toward others (sexism, racism, and excessive nationalism are the most flagrant cultural values) simply because they are operating out of a culture that accepts such views and they have a superego that sanctions such thinking. Only conscience, rooted in the nurturing experience of parental care and fostered by the thrust of empathic sensitivity, can sunder the stranglehold that the superego subtly holds on even genuinely good people.

This short explanation of the superego's tie to culture goes a long way in explaining the adolescent's struggle to fashion a moral self that is other-centered. Not only must the adolescent contend with developmental insecurities which often lead the adolescent to take refuge in stereotypic attitudes but the adolescent has internalized through the years a wide variety of unreflected attitudes and perceptions that forestall if not preclude at times the forming of an other-centered value sense that is caring and compassionate. Thus, the adolescent (like everyone else) is, in a sense, handicapped. He or she is apt to be capable at times of great generosity and self-sacrifice, yet at other times display genuinely selfish, narrowing, and at times harsh judgments and hostile behaviors toward others.

Eli Sagan highlights the eternal war between the superego and the conscience by recalling one of American literature's most famous adolescents, Huckleberry Finn. Huckleberry flees the family home and his sick and sadistic father. He encounters along the way a runaway slave, Jim. We are treated in Twain's writing to the internal debate that takes place in Huck between his superego, which tells him to send Jim back to his master, Miss Watson, and his conscience, which fights for his freedom. Huck wrestles within between his struggling desire to proclaim the other-centered values of compassion and love as he grew in his own friendship with Jim, and the opposing call of his superego for obedience and order and the need to send Jim back "where he belonged." In the end, Huck's conscience triumphs. He tears up the letter he is writing to Miss Watson. Sagan, in commenting on Huck's dilemma, notes insightfully that Huck's "actions can be accurately described as *feeling guilty about behaving morally*. This irony clearly demonstrates that something is radically wrong with a theory that equates morality and superego."[10] Huck felt guilty about what he did. Ironically, the truly moral action elicits guilt. Again, we see the power of the superego.

This leads us to the last feature of the superego that disqualifies it as the source for morality. The guilt which arises from the superego has the potential for being cruel and vindictive. In a sense, superego guilt is blind as it wages its attack on one's personal character and self-esteem. The guilt of the superego is extraordinarily punitive, often blind to the realities of actual transgressions. One need only to listen to the stories told by many adults of their sexual feelings to witness the ravages of superego guilt. The consequences of superego guilt are often crippling, leading many to assuage their guilt through overdependency ("I will always rely on you and depend on you no matter what you do") or a pervasive feeling of low self-esteem ("No matter what I do I'm no good"). An example of such guilt is the child of an alcoholic parent who mistakenly believes that he or she could somehow have "saved" the parent from alcoholism. Even as adults (adult children of alcoholics) these children find themselves burdened by dependency needs, continually trying to please others or seek acceptance because of their own emotionally impoverished upbringing. Superego guilt, in such instances, is tyrannical and ravages the child's psychological health.

It needs to be stated that a focus on "right and wrong," on "rules and regulations," does have an *invaluable* place in moral education. Most certainly, the adolescent is in need of guidance and the setting down of rules to govern behavior. Moreover, a critical component of adolescent moral development is the active presence of adult authority, which serves as a valuable resource and provides needed boundaries and input (feedback) for the adolescent's moral search. Nevertheless, the prohibitions and demands framed by the superego are limiting. That is, the superego reflects neither a moral vision of the future, a deepening interpersonal communion that is realized in social bonding, nor a creative incorporation of experiences that invites and sustains a maturing sense of responsible selfhood, both of which are necessary to healthy adolescent moral development.

A way to enhance the distinction between superego and conscience (as we have envisioned it as the source and discerning force for other-centered value) is to pose some pastoral questions which evolve from each perspective.

A pastoral approach emanating from the superego is focused on "What did you do wrong?" A conscience approach, while acknowledging personal transgressions, seeks to aid the adolescent in discovering what he or she has learned from this experience and what the future might hold in light of this experience. Thus questions which a conscience approach might pose include, "Now that this experience has taken place, what do you think you have learned about yourself?" "How are you different because of this experience?" "What does this teach you about yourself in order that you might better be prepared to be who you truly want to be?" (An aspect of this discussion would be the ideals to which the adolescent aspires.)

A superego approach to pastoral care, likewise, focuses on punishment and retribution: "How are you going to make up for this mistake?" On the other hand, the conscience approach acknowledges the need for justice, yet it seeks to foster self-insight and a reflective sense of value development: "What do you think led you to do this?" "As you reflect on your life, how does this experience compare with who you are and what you want to be?" "What do you think influences you to be like this?"

Finally, the superego commonly addresses questions of law: "You broke the law!" "What you did was wrong!" "We have to obey." Conscience respects law and rules yet it seeks to discover the wisdom behind the rule and the common communal bonding that requires caring and sensitive behavior. Thus, questions it elicits are, "Why do you think there is such a rule?" "How do you think the other person feels?" "Who has been hurt and why?"

An example is helpful. A college freshman (we will call her Janet) is seriously involved in a relationship. Recently, however, she finds the relationship increasingly distressful and frustrating and breaks up with her boyfriend. In discussing this relationship it surfaces that this relationship has been a maturing experience for Janet. Yet, it is also clear that some aspects of the relationship show a darker side. The relationship involved control and jealousy. Manipulation of the other was acknowledged as well as the need for control. In retrospect, as Janet reflects on this relationship she feels very ambivalent. In this example, the conscience approach would attempt to engage the adolescent in a discussion of the values that this relationship reflected. In addition, it would acknowledge the need for growth and forgiveness. Also, it would seek to aid the adolescent in reflecting on how this experience has touched her personal sense of who she is as a moral person and what this relationship might mean in terms of future relationships. Finally, a worthy topic of discussion are the ideals by which Janet seeks to live her life and the extent to which her behaviors might strive to reflect these ideals.

Obviously, to endorse the view of a conscience approach requires a tremendous amount of patience on the part of the adult. Likewise, it entails time and energy rather than a quick response to complex pastoral questions; essentially, it is a dialogue and requires a certain capacity for reflection on the adolescent's part. As such it is more suitable for middle and late adolescents. Nonetheless, in terms of pastoral effectiveness, it is the single, most promising approach. That is, it is the approach that offers the adolescent the optimal opportunity to reflect on his or her values, recognize the need for ongoing growth, and integrate his or her experiences with the growth of a personal and authentic moral vision.

Conscience, then, may be viewed as separate from the super-ego. As noted previously, a Christian view of conscience points to its other-centeredness and deepening capacity to incorporate such values in everyday life decisions.

How might such a view of conscience operate in the life of the adolescent? I propose that conscience which is viewed as other-centered value incorporates seven dimensions that serve as the basis for the ongoing dynamic of the adolescent's development of the moral self. The task before us is to examine how each of these dimensions functions in the adolescent's life. It is to this task that we now turn.

Adaptive Psychic Energy

The demands of physical-neurological growth and the presence of internal needs leads the infant to seek increasingly adaptive yet gratifying forms of behavior. When we observe infants and children we cannot help but be fascinated by the immense repertoire of psychophysically based reactions that blend together to foster adaptive functioning. It is possible, for instance, to view the child's growth from a variety of bipolar perspectives: active/passive; negative/positive mood; responsive/withdrawing; consistent/inconsistent; content/discontented. These "stylistic" approaches to the environment—as well as other temperamental characteristics such as impulsivity and emotionality—blend with biological development, social interactions, and learned behavior to create for each child a "unique" approach to life. As such, we can argue that there exists, at least to some extent, a biological basis for morality. In sum, the model we propose is a biopsychosocial model that employs the perspectives of the physical, emotional-mental, and social worlds. Through this blending the child, ideally, comes to master his or her environment and to forge an adequate sense of self-esteem. The unique approach of each child to his or her world helps to shape the environment in which the child lives. At the same time, the environment within which the child lives conditions the child's distinct and unique approach, thereby creating an interplay of interaction between the self and the environment that leads to ongoing development.

By the adolescent years, the child's "unique" approach to the world is firmly in place. How does the adolescent's mode of adaptation to the world influence the development of conscience? There are several ways in which this can be explored. First, psychic energy represents the psychological fuel for adaptive life functioning and sustains one's style for negotiating and functioning in life. In order for conscience to function, there must exist, by necessity, an adequate amount of psychic energy. Psychic energy, in short, is required for all psychological activity. It is, in other words, the source for the psyche's life. Thus, emotions, dreams, reflection, attachment, and so on are impossible without the presence of psychic energy. As noted above, there exists a uniqueness to each child's approach to life. One child's style may lead to an impulsive mode of action whereas another child's style might be withdrawn or methodical. Every stylistic approach is fashioned through countless interactions with significant others and with the environment at large; the approach in turn influences conscience and the development of moral values.

> Thus, conscience and moral values are not elemental psychological faculties, but involve and depend on a number of cognitive and affective functions. Morality, therefore, will "take," flourish, and, in turn, influence and possibly contribute to various more general aspects of the overall style in certain contexts.[11]

The adolescent utilizes psychic energy within a distinctive approach to life; this is best expressed as the capacity to attend and focus. In other words, the adolescent's adaptive style, which is fueled through the expenditure of psychic energy, is best expressed by examining the adolescent's "focus of attention." We noted two features of the adolescent's attention (or what we might term *conscious experience*). First, attention requires activity. That is, we must orient and focus ourselves in order to do anything. Thus "the way adolescents' attention is allocated—what they attend to, how intensely, and for how long—delimits their potential for growth and range of their life accomplishments."[12] The second feature of attention is the simple fact that it is limited. One has only a limited amount of energy, which necessitates choosing certain desires, goals, pursuits and giving up others. "The opportunities for growth have finite bounds, and adolescents must choose which pattern to actualize by investing their attention into it."[13] Obviously, if psychic energy was limitless, few problems would occur for adolescents or anyone else. In such a scenario, a person could eventually if not immediately satisfy all meaningful goals and pursuits. However, the limited nature of psychic energy poses challenges. Given the developmental tasks of this age period (for example, establishing a personal identify, acquiring career goals, developing an initial philosophy of life), the futile pursuit of distracting and potentially risky behaviors such as drug taking or even a seemingly innocuous activity such as excessive television watching are serious concerns.

In sum, adaptive psychic functioning involves responsive and responsible attentiveness on the adolescent's part. Attention focuses the adolescent on constructive endeavors, thereby allowing for the optimal completion of developmental tasks. Positive use of attention enhances the forming of a developed conscience. A healthy focus on career goals, maturing and positive attachments, the resolution of moral conflicts and dilemmas, as well as numerous other experiences are natural recipients of the adolescent's attention. In turn it is these very experiences that lead the adolescent to discover a deepening sense of other-centered value and a growing capacity for maturative moral decision making. For example, attending to such a necessary developmental need as friendship formation engages the adolescent in a variety of ways. Relationships allow the adolescent the opportunity to explore previously unacknowledged feelings while they foster self-esteem. A developing friendship provides the adolescent with necessary reassurance that he or she is valued. Furthermore, inevitable conflicts and compromises that emanate from friendship encourage the working out of ethical values and the need to explore attitudes and previously untested assumptions. A basic ingredient in any friendship is the presence of trust and the requirement to honor confidences. The result of healthy friendship attachment is self-knowledge and greater openness to others. To be sure, many adolescent experiences of friendship are not positive. All too often adolescent attachments are subject to exploitation, unhealthy dependency, or the collusion of the two immature selves in nongrowthful and immature forms of behavior. Yet, when they are healthy, attachments contribute to the forming of conscience.

Although there exists no exact "set" of goals that the adolescent must achieve, it is reasonable to conclude that some essential goals must be envisioned for the high school and college under-graduate years. Among these goals are

1. acceptance of one's physical self and personal limitations,
2. developing a philosophy of life and meaningful ethical code to guide personal behavior,
3. acquiring an adequate knowledge of the social and political world,
4. defining oneself as man or woman in modern society,
5. developing sustained commitments in terms of friendships with both sexes,
6. preparing for vocational choice, and
7. fostering hobbies, interests, and other projects that enhance one's skills and self-knowledge.

One thing we note from any list like the one above is that it demands an extended time period: that is, the successful comple-tion of these tasks preoccupies all phases of the adolescent period (early, middle, late, and often the young adult years). Moreover, a listing of the tasks adolescents must complete provides insight into why this period for many adolescents can be stressful and confus-ing. Indeed, some adolescents feel overwhelmed by the demands of this age period. Adolescents who expend their psychic energies without attending to these necessary aspects of development find difficulty in achieving the self-reflection and maturity that are nec-essary for moral decision making.

Defensive Psychic Functioning

As the adolescent adapts to the environment, he or she needs to acquire the psychological tools to deal with such anxiety-provoking experiences as loss and disappointment, as well as to re-solve constructively issues related to thwarted needs and internal conflicts. Defense mechanisms are psychological responses that the self utilizes to deal with anxiety and threats to the ego's self-esteem. Central to the adaptive capacity of the person, then, is not only the proper focusing of psychic energy but also the capacity for utilizing psychological resources that allow one to cope with the numerous psychic threats of everyday life.

Among the first of these threatening experiences is the infant's gradual separation from the mother and the development of an essential trust. Erikson has noted that the first psychological test for the child (what he terms a crisis) occurs with the child's need to experience an essential level of trust in the parent-child bond. This formation of trust is continually challenged by the anxieties and frustrations that accompany the separation-individuation struggles of the child's early years. Through this process of separation (which can be defined as the infant's growing realization of a self as distinct from the mother) and individuation (the ongoing development of the infant's cognitive, biological, and emotional capacities) there emerges a growing and cohesive sense of self that sustains the child's developing mastery of the environment as well as an increasing capacity for purposeful and autonomous behavior. As the child develops there occurs not only the need to integrate positive and negative feelings (which arise from separation-individuation struggles), but the parallel need to master social rules. The growing demands of the child's environment challenge the more egotistical framework through which the child originally envisions the world, thereupon necessitating the formation of defense mechanisms that provide the child with a reliable shield for deflecting unacceptable levels of frustration, disillusionment, and inner conflict.

Defense mechanisms in children are less adaptive than those of adults. One common defense mechanism frequently used by children is regression (acting in immature ways). An example of this defense is the ten-year-old child who throws a tantrum when he or she does not get his or her way. Another defense mechanism is somatization. This defense is employed when the child expresses emotional conflicts through physical illness. The child who complains of constant stomach trouble, for example, might well be suffering from depression or experiencing psychological conflict. Another common childhood defense is acting out, which occurs when the child's internal psychological distress is "acted out" through overt behavior. There exist numerous other defense mechanisms that children often use. These include projection, denial, displacement, and reaction formation.[14]

In general, adults utilize more mature defense mechanisms. Mature defensive functioning is a sign of psychological health and reflects an adaptive, flexible approach to life as well as the satisfactory resolution of internal psychic conflicts. As one might expect, healthy adults will periodically resort to immature defense functioning. A likely time to observe this phenomenon is when the adult is under stress or suffering from severe psychological conflict. For example, an adult who is under severe stress at work and is experiencing conflict in his marriage might resort to projection in order to cope with psychic stress. Thus he might project unacknowledged feelings on to his spouse as a way to resolve increasing tension and hostility toward her.

As the bridge between childhood and adulthood, adolescence is a period of life that exhibits a wide variety of defenses. In essence, the adolescent must again separate from the parents and begin to face the demands of adulthood. In order to cope with these stresses, the adolescent will periodically employ, particularly in the early and middle adolescent years, less adaptive (immature) defenses. This tendency reflects the child's own immaturity and the lack of adequate means of coping with the developmental challenges of adolescence. As adolescence proceeds, a more mature defensive functioning emerges. Indeed, the employment of mature defenses reflects growing psychological maturity.

There are several defense mechanisms which signify healthy adult functioning and adaptation. Healthy adolescent growth increasingly incorporates these defenses as ways to modulate developmental stresses and internal conflicts. Increasingly mature defense mechanisms allow the adolescent to respond to others in developmentally appropriate ways, thereby insuring the forming of relational commitments that invite the growing acceptance of other-centered values.

Several mature defenses employed in the adolescent years are critical for conscience formation. A brief description of each is given below.

Sublimation: The biological changes adolescents undergo and the increasing demands of identity acquisition lead to inevitable conflict over impulse control, particularly the control and responsible use of sexuality.

> While much is made nowadays of sexual liberation, there is another side to teenage sexual life—the constant struggle of millions of youths for a reliable sense of control over their emotions, including their sexual urges. The achievement of that control is necessary in any life, lest a man or woman become plagued by impulsiveness.[15]

In order to invest themselves productively within society, adolescents are in need of constructive outlets within which to channel their needs and desires. Sublimation refers to the substituting of accepted behaviors for one's aggressive, sexual, and inappropriate emotional expressions. These substitutions range from hobbies and socially accepted interests to very individualized efforts (for example, training for a sports event or creative writing). The fruits of successful sublimation are the channeling of psychic energy into meaningful and productive activities. This results in not only a lessening of psychic conflicts and frustration but also the building of self-esteem through the accomplishment of socially accepted goals.

An essential component of sublimation is the reliance on creativity and imagination. Successful sublimation requires motivation and resourcefulness. These qualities serve to instill within the adolescent a growing sense of self-mastery and the capacity successfully to resolve internal sources of tension and frustration. The self-control and self-reliance that sublimation reinforces creates for the adolescent the opportunity to experience a felt sense of virtue; that is, prudence and hope are more easily expressed when there is the ongoing experience of meaningful creativity that opens for the adolescent new vistas for maturing self-expression and healthy identity growth. Together these growing capacities invite a deepening level of freedom through the control of impulses and the authentic expression of talents and energies. Sublimation, consequently, is a welcome ally that allows the adolescent to experience conscience as a liberating focus.

Altruism: Caring for others provides a socially acceptable way to further interpersonal trust and enhance self-esteem. Acts of generosity and sacrifice help the adolescent to explore his or her own growing sensitivities. Furthermore, altruism serves as a direct counter to aggressive impulses and the more self-centered concerns that preoccupy many adolescents. At the same time, some caution is warranted when discussing the adolescent's altruistic response. When taken to extremes, altruism can signify a compulsive caregiving approach to others.[16] An example of such an approach is the adolescent who continually places the interests and concerns of others above his or her own legitimate needs and welfare. In such instances, what passes for altruism more likely reflects inadequate self-esteem and deep insecurities. As such, this misdirected care giving is an attempt to assuage inner psychic feelings of "badness" or "fill up" what the adolescent experiences as an internal void rather than an authentic reflection of altruism, which is a caring response to the needs of others. Utilizing the defense of altruism requires a sufficient level of self-esteem and healthy attachment. Only the adolescent who experiences such positive feelings is capable of attending adequately to the needs and hurts of others and be capable of freely sacrificing personal interest for the other's welfare. As is obvious, the commitment to an altruistic defense expands the scope of conscience through reinforcing the priority of love and the expression of other-centered values.

Humor: Humor can be an extremely positive defense. For one, it allows the adolescent to broach heretofore forbidden areas of discussion. Further, it diffuses the anxiety and self-consciousness that accompany adolescent maturation. As such, humor enhances the adolescent's social standing and can be a welcome ally in the formation of friendships. Emotional conflicts and sexual anxieties are threats that can be eased by a good sense of humor. Moreover, humor serves as a disengaging mechanism inasmuch as it distances the adolescent from overinvolvement in personal concerns. In other words, a healthy sense of humor allows the adolescent to view himself or herself in a playful and self-critical fashion, thereby discouraging overinvestment of the self and the inevitable blindness to self-reflection that comes from a narrow focus. The freedom with which humor invests conscience fosters the capacity for mature self-examination. Yet adolescent humor can be a destructive force when used to attack directly the self-esteem or needs of others. Often adolescents employ humor as a means for self-aggrandizement at the expense of others. Profitable strategies for assessing the psychological (and moral) health of humor center on the question, Does the humor you use build up others and allow you to be a more loving person? The less this question can be answered in the affirmative, the more likely that humor is being employed in a narrowing and nonadaptive way. With this question as a guideline, adults would do well to explore with adolescents their use of humor.

Role flexibility: Whereas adaptive defense mechanisms for adults focus on the experience of commitment and the building of sustained and enduring life goals, the adolescent experience of commitment is more likely viewed as a gradual and tentative response which sows the seeds for later commitments. As was pointed out in an earlier chapter, adolescents take on a variety of roles and live them out with newfound intensity. An adolescent son or daughter comes to deeper realization of what this role is as he or she renegotiates the meaning of relating to parents. The role of friends is felt with newfound intensity as emotional experiences are more acutely felt. Roles such as worker, student, or club member take on added meanings. In all of these roles, each of which must be continually negotiated, the adolescent is challenged to view his or her capacity for commitment in preparation for adulthood. At the same time, commitments such as marriage or vocation that are undertaken prematurely or with little preparation lead to foreclosure in self-identity, whereas the inability to make commitments render the adolescent subject to a diffuse psychological state in which little direction or life purpose exists. Role flexibility encourages the development of conscience through the evolving discernment of the values required for various roles. Questions of fidelity, honesty, and self-sacrifice are essential for enduring commitment; a variety of roles offers the adolescent an opportunity to learn mature moral responses.

Suppression: The defense mechanism of suppression refers to "the conscious or semiconscious decision to postpone attention to a conscious impulse or conflict."[17] Naturally, this defense exercises a critical role in adolescent development. As noted previously, a continual challenge for the adolescent is the mastery of impulse (which includes the belief on the adolescent's part that impulses can be controlled). The use of suppression allows the young person to portion needed time and energies for productive pursuits thereby encouraging emotional development. The inability to suppress impulses results in lingering immaturity. It might be helpful to view suppression as an internal psychic mechanism and the capacity for self-control as its behavioral correlate. Appropriate use of this defense solidifies the young person's capacity to temper impulses and act responsibly. Further, the use of suppression provides the adolescent with increasing opportunities to explore alternative options to impulsive responses thus encouraging dependable and consistent behavior, a sense of self-mastery, opportunity for reflection and evaluation of personal behaviors—all vital ingredients in a healthy functioning conscience.

The above brief descriptions provide a summary of adaptive defense responses. From my own clinical-pastoral experience, I would say that adolescents employ a variety of defense mechanisms that are distinctly maladapted. These immature defenses frustrate growth and inhibit the formation of conscience. We examine these defenses below.

Minimalization: This defense seeks to limit the importance or significance of a moral conflict: for example, the question of honesty which the adolescent minimalizes in a relationship in order to avoid facing personal responsibility. In effect, minimalization serves as a buffer against the responsible use of freedom and provides for the adolescent a ready invitation for self-deception.

Totalism: Totalism is the adolescent's self-absorbtion in one activity or pursuit to the neglect of other responsibilities. A preoccupation with a fad, overinvolvement in sports or a relationship, and so on can all serve to mask insecurities. In addition, overpreoccupation renders the adolescent ill-equipped to look dispassionately and maturely at his or her personal behaviors and hinders the acknowledgment of value conflicts and the awareness of value.

Externalization: One of the most commonly used defenses of adults as well as adolescents, externalization refers to the blaming of someone else for one's own transgressions. Although this defense has several definitions, I use it to mean the adolescent's all too frequent willingness to reproach parents and other adults rather than admit personal responsibility for actions.

Intellectualization: This mechanism is employed when the adolescent distances himself or herself from the emotional significance of events. The problem with this defense is that it inhibits the affective dimensions of conscience and creates a constricted, simplistic, and narrow view of values as rules.

Inhibition: For some adolescents, life dilemmas are not viewed in the context of attempting to control often unmanageable impulses; rather, there exists an overcontrol of impulses. In such instances, conscience is deprived of opportunities to struggle with and resolve issues of value conflict and personal responsibility.

Acting Out: In order to avoid facing internal conflicts and the anxiety they provoke, some adolescents will simply act out their conflicts in unruly and unacceptable ways. Such expressions are an attempt to avoid facing troubling emotions. From the perspective of conscience formation, the significance of acting out resides in the encouragement it gives an impulsive and unreflective style that undermines the deliberative and reflective sense needed for maturity and conscience formation.

Rationalization: Simply stated, rationalizing is the making of excuses. More specifically, it reflects the tendency to explain irresponsible, nongrowthful, and immoral behavior in ways that exonerate the adolescent from taking responsibility for his or her action.

Compartmentalizing: This defense concerns the excluding of certain areas of one's life from self-examination. A classic example of this is the adolescent who is involved in a sexual relationship yet refuses to explore the moral questions or value expressions involved. At the same time, he or she consciously reflects on other areas of his or her life. In effect, the adolescent is compartmentalizing a vital area of life, thereby sealing it off from serious examination.

Stereotyping: Stereotyping refers to the tendency to deny individual differences or the simple fact that others might be different and that their difference is, indeed, legitimate. Adolescents are notorious for stereotyping. Another peer group, an outsider, another school's sports team, or another race or culture can be subject to the adolescent's scorn and criticism. Stereotyping exists because the adolescent fears the unknown. Although on the one hand adolescents seek to venture forth and discover new aspects of life and of their own selves, on the other hand they often retreat to the safety of their own preconceived opinions and judgments as a way to lessen insecurity and self-doubt. Stereotyping prevents the possibility of more deeply discovering the reality of a situation and the corresponding discovery of values and challenges that new situations provide for self-reflection and growth.

The adolescent's overuse of immature defense mechanisms leads to several undesirable results. First, reality is to various degrees distorted. Second, the adolescent avoids needed self-examination (this avoidance is a prime goal of maladapted defenses). Third, moral growth is readily compromised. And last, defenses limit possibilities for the emotional maturation that is necessary for human as well as moral growth.

Empathy.

A third psychological dimension necessary for conscience formation is empathy. We can view empathy as the emotional foundation for conscience. We have noted that the nature of the maturing, healthy conscience requires the development of other-centeredness. Empathy provides the human capacity needed for responding to another and the human sensitivity for bonding. A way to conceptualize empathic experience is to view it as the psychological glue—the critical psychological ingredient—that leads to enduring attachment. Empathy is defined as a vicarious emotional arousal to the experience of the other. Usually, this view of empathy has been studied in terms of one's distress when empathizing with the pain and hurts of the other.

Psychologist Martin Hoffman has set forth a sophisticated theory of empathy's development.[18] According to Hoffman, empathy has three components: cognitive, emotional, and motivational. Hoffman's theory focuses on empathic arousal, which is experienced when one empathizes with the pain and hurts of others. As such, his view of empathy offers a distinctively caring flavor that is fundamentally altruistic in nature. In other words, Hoffman's understanding of empathy is easily reconciled with notions of empathy that stress selfless love and care. Each of empathy's components arises from the interaction of normal maturation and the resources arising from a positive environment. Empathy reaches its highest level of maturation during the adolescent years. The development of its three components provides the essential foundation for maturative interpersonal functioning characterized by compassion and service to others.

A short description of each empathy component is given below.

Cognition: A commonsense understanding of empathy might lead one to the conclusion that empathy is solely an emotional experience. On the contrary, it is to Hoffman's credit that he has pointed out the crucial role of cognition for empathic development. Cognition enables the empathizer to discern a situation accurately. Without an accurate perception, one could not respond in an appropriate fashion. For example, if one views a situation where a person is suffering and correctly interprets the cause of his or her plight—say, a crippling sickness or an unforeseen misfortune—then one is most apt to respond empathically and be vicariously aroused to the other's adversity. This accurate perception is the cognitive component; it is an essential component for any empathic response. Furthermore, it is this accurate perception and interpretation of the situation that allows one to respond compassionately. For the sake of contrast, if one interpreted the adverse circumstances of another as resulting from the person's own selfish motives or irresponsible behavior, then one would be much less likely to respond to another's pain and hurt.

From a developmental perspective, cognition provides for increasingly accurate evaluations of situations, thereby fostering a more appropriate empathic response. For example, an eighteen-month-old child is unable to differentiate his or her internal state from another person's needs: in effect, he or she believes that everyone feels in a similar way. Consequently, the toddler who perceives another child as crying is most apt to respond to the other child's distress by offering his or her own toy to the upset child. The child giving the toy is unable to comprehend that the distressed child might not find the toy comforting. In effect, the comprehension of another's feeling during these years is essentially egotistic; that is, there is a fundamental inability to assess accurately the feelings of another. The child who offers the toy incorrectly assumes that every child would find such a toy a soothing distraction. Thus the child is unable to appreciate the separate need states of others and mistakenly assumes the other's need states are similar to his or her own needs. As the childhood years progress, children are capable of more accurate interpretations of situations and more correct understanding of the wishes and needs of others, as well as the realization that other's needs can be unlike their own. This maturing cognitive sense allows for more accurate empathic responding. In sum, empathic responding is clearly present during the early years, yet it is expressed (and limited) by the developmental level at which one can accurately interpret and understand another's life situation.

A critical cognitive dimension of empathy surfaces, however, with the advent of adolescence. We noted in chapter 1 that an increasing level of abstraction is characteristic of adolescent cognitive development. Having obtained this abstractive capacity, the adolescent is capable of comprehending the plight and suffering of large classes of people (for example, the poor or victims of disaster). A child of eight may watch a television show and become upset when viewing scenes that portray starvation in Africa. Most likely, the child's empathic distress is focused on the concrete picture he or she views on the screen. By contrast, an adolescent who views the same sequences on television can empathize not only with the people on the screen, but also with the distant masses who are not pictured but who are malnourished. Furthermore, the adolescent can more correctly interpret the actual situation in the beleaguered country—the causes for the hunger and what can actually be done to alleviate it. In short, Hoffman has noted that this abstract capacity, which arises only with the advent of adolescent formal thinking, is a vital dimension of fully developed empathic responding.

Emotion: One's visceral arousal to the hurts and needs of others (the internal distress the empathizer feels on perceiving the pain of another) represents the emotional component of empathy. This emotional arousal is characterized by a physiological response and a felt sense of distress. An individual who feels empathic distress reports the feeling of being "uncomfortable." He or she is uneasy and preoccupied with the other's pain. There is often a vicarious feeling of the other's hurt. The most likely response to these unsettled feelings is some attempt to address the cause of the sufferer's distress or alleviate the pain the sufferer experiences.

One might speculate as to what happens when one is empathically aroused to another's hurt and is unable to offer comfort or redress the wrong that has caused the suffering. Such individuals, over time, may become emotionally overwhelmed and subject to burnout. In the long run, the human biological system is unable to sustain continuous emotional distress (empathic overarousal) and, over time, one will slowly disengage from stress-induced situations. Consequently, health-care providers and professionals in ministry who are exposed continually to acute instances of others suffering must develop mature and effective coping skills in order to deal with their distress.

Some adolescents are at times unable to respond appropriately to their own empathic stirrings and therefore seek to deny their empathic experiences. When this occurs, they most likely utilize the defense of denial or acting out in order to avoid the acute feeling of empathic distress. A very common example of this is the adolescent who views someone suffering and who makes statements like "it is their own fault, why don't they work" or "they could have prevented it." In this instance, the adolescent is often shielding himself or herself from experiencing an empathic reaction toward those who are suffering. The adolescent is simply uncomfortable with internal feelings of vulnerability, tenderness, and distress.

Motivation: As noted above, empathic arousal tends heavily toward responses that alleviate the other's suffering. Hence, there exists a compassionate flavor to empathy that usually leads to altruism. In other words, having vicariously experienced the hurt and pain of others, the empathizer is apt to respond in a way that alleviates the other's pain and hurt.

Empathy is vital for sound interpersonal functioning. Because relationships are so crucial for healthy emotional growth, empathy, naturally, is indispensable. Still, some circumspection is necessary when we focus on the adolescent experience. Overempathizing with another can foster overly intense and precipitous attempts at psychic merger (the blurring of identities). Adolescents experience a recapitulation of the separation-individuation struggles that occur in the child's early years. The psychic resources necessary to deal with these struggles are often eased by overidentification with others and intense emotional investment with peers. The adolescent struggling with self-identity discovers that investing psychically in intense relationships provides solace from acutely troubled feelings. However, such intense involvement can blur the boundaries necessary for mature decision making and healthy relationships. In sum, empathy is a vital component for the psychology of conscience. The emotions exercise a pivotal role in any response to another and, above all, the capacity for empathy orients one to respond with the sensitivity that expresses authentic other-centered value. Yet, the capacity for empathy must be experienced in light of sufficiently mature identity functioning in order that empathic responses are both behaviorally appropriate and a true indication of the adolescent's inner freedom.

Guilt

Guilt responses are an integral dimension of conscience. Unfortunately, guilt is too often viewed in a negative way. It is true that experiences of guilt can be debilitating. The consequences of unhealthy guilt are often crippling. They include weakened self-esteem, depression, a sense of personal devaluation, and compensating behaviors which often take on a compulsive quality.

A necessary goal for every adolescent is developing ways to constructively deal with the painful effects of guilt. Some adolescents attack guilt head on through reckless disregard of rules and appropriate behaviors. In such instances, the adolescent is attempting to deny his or her own feelings of guilt. Other adolescents (and adults) will become obsessively preoccupied with thoughts and behaviors which serve to ward off their never-ending guilt feelings.

Unhealthy guilt emanates from the superego. As noted previously, when we described the distinction between superego and conscience we noted that the superego is wedded to external sources of authority, is overly punitive, and is embedded in the past.

Superego guilt is inevitably enervating, for it slowly diminishes psychic resources, thereby inhibiting the adolescent's investment in productive and growth-oriented pursuits. As such, superego guilt reactions are by their very nature unavoidably "entropic" experiences. Recall that entropy is the scientific term referring to the inevitable breakdown and loss that occurs in any existing and functioning body or system. Superego guilt is the debilitating experience which over time leads inexorably to inefficiency in behavior and growing self-devaluation which impinges not only on the self but on interpersonal functioning.

Hoffman has speculated on the development of the guilt experience and its critical role in the formation of caring behavior.[19] From the perspective he outlines, guilt can be considered a natural and healthy component in the development of attachment and exercises a vital role in interpersonal functioning. (I term this experience of guilt *moral guilt* in order to distinguish it from the superego guilt defined above.)

Evidence points to the fact that individuals feel guilty over initiating behaviors that are injurious to others. This feeling is experienced as a sense of devaluation, a weakening of self-esteem, or a generalized sense of inner turmoil. Equally important, these guilt feelings lead one to respond to another in a reparative fashion that offers some type of retribution for the wrong incurred. It is to Hoffman's credit that he has been able to distill these positive aspects of guilt in terms of a developmental process of growth similar to empathic development which was outlined above.

According to Hoffman, guilt, like empathy, has three components: cognitive, affective, and motivational. The cognitive dimension of guilt includes the awareness of another as a thinking and feeling person. It also includes the realization that one has harmed another. From a cognitive perspective, being aware that one has harmed another is most likely the easiest form of guilt to experience. More demanding is realizing that one "could have" done something to aid another; in other words, an act of omission requires more cognitive effort than the experience of having hurt another. Further cognitive sophistication is required to experience guilt associated with the thought that one "could have" done something. To feel this guilt one admits the connection among one's intentions, thoughts, and the possibility of action. Another part of the cognitive dimension of guilt "is the awareness that one has a choice and control over one's behavior."[20] One further dimension of guilt occurs when one realizes the rules and norms of society which forbid the harming of others. When one violates such rules one's own self-image is threatened, thereby engendering emotional distress. All in all, the end result of moral guilt is often repair of the injury one has caused another and a response of solace and support.

Just as the adolescent period sets the stage for experiencing the most advanced form of empathy, the adolescent years provide the setting for a special kind of guilt that Hoffman labels "existential guilt." In instances where one compares one's own advantages to the more disadvantaged state of another, even though one has done nothing directly to harm another, one may feel guilty. A classic example is the middle or late adolescent from middle- or upper-class origins who, through classroom instruction or study, begins to feel guilty about his or her advantaged state when compared to the plight of minorities and disadvantaged classes. Such guilt requires the presence of formal thinking and a certain level of empathic distress. Obviously this capacity for existential guilt has important consequences for the development of a social justice orientation. (I have speculated elsewhere on the nature of empathy and social justice education.[21])

The importance of Hoffman's perspective is that it offers guilt as a vital component in the development of the caring behavior that is critical for the development of conscience as other-centered value. Moral guilt serves as a vital linchpin in orienting one to awareness of personal transgressions and the need for forgiveness. Furthermore, such guilt induces a response that is caring and sensitive to the concerns of others.

Admittedly, the experience of guilt is one of the most difficult psychological tightropes to walk. That is, if experienced too intensely its effects can be crippling. On the other hand, to deny the experience of guilt deprives the self of a naturally occurring psychic experience whose function nourishes sensitivity and altruistic responding. Maintaining a proper balance concerning guilt is difficult at any age, and all the more difficult during adolescence: the young person may deny guilt because it looms as overwhelmingly threatening or may surrender to guilt because of insufficient ego strength. I have found that the most adequate pastoral response to adolescent guilt reactions is to support the adolescent in acknowledging and taking responsibility for personal transgressions while focusing not on what has happened but on what the future can become, on how their future lives might be different, on what they can do for others in light of their current failings, and on how their increasing self-knowledge from their present experience will aid them in responding more appropriately in the future.

Idealization

In chapter 2 we defined the ego ideal as the agent of aspiration that reflects our values. In the evolution of Freud's thought, the ego ideal, like the conscience, became subsumed under the psychic structure known as the superego. More recent psychoanalytic thinking has attempted to distill the individuality of the ego ideal as a separate psychic structure.

The ego ideal occupies a unique role in the development of the psychology of conscience. As noted, we have defined conscience as the agency of other-centered value which forges compassionate sensitivity. An integral aspect of conscience, then, is its thrust toward the future, its capacity to appropriate increasingly a sense of care. Psychoanalyst Chasseguet-Smirgel captures the essence of the ego ideal when she notes that "the ego ideal implies the idea of a *project*."[22] This "project," encapsulated in the human capacity for

89

personal striving, reflects an essential commitment to hope. That is, one's capacity to sustain effort and personal commitment in an endeavor, reflects a positive thrust in one's ability to create a favorable outcome. The fundamental consequence of such an orientation is an anticipation of the future and a sustained confidence in one's pursuits. As such, "project and hope imply postponement, delay, a temporal perspective."[23]

Translated into psychological experience, human effort might be viewed as the following: The ego ideal is the central organizing mechanism that looks beyond one's present mode of existence and increasingly appropriates more maturative tasks and goals. Initially, the child, as a consequence of his or her disillusionment at the realization of not being the all-powerful center of the world, projects the desire for idealization on parental and other adult figures. However, as development proceeds, the child comes to differentiate other sources of pleasure and proceeds to individuate through the gradual mastery of developmental tasks. Each accomplishment (whether it be crawling, walking, or speaking) forms a greater source for idealization and personal self-esteem. Each task successfully mastered serves as a source for self-validation. In this ongoing developmental thrust the child must experience sufficient gratification, yet not be so content that he or she is unmotivated to proceed further to increasing levels of self-mastery, and correspondingly to seek more mature ideals. Throughout this process the child must acquire an adequate sense of frustration tolerance, yet continually be oriented to aspire beyond his or her present circumstances. Developmentally, particularly with the advent of adolescence, these aspirations (idealizations) take more sophisticated form and are soon channeled into projects that entail more accomplished and maturing efforts. By the adolescent years, these aspirations find their home in idealized relationships. An adolescent might idealize a teacher or professor. Likewise, there is the search and experience of the "perfect" friendship or the adolescent "crush" on a sports hero or rock star. Idealizations are also lived out through sustained efforts (making the sports team or becoming its star) or personal goals (creative efforts in art or science). These idealizations are reflected in the adolescent's investment in specific causes or a project which takes on intense personal meaning. In such instances, the adolescent seeks to experience a sense of power and self-satisfaction through the extolling of and investing in an ideal.

Inevitably, many adolescent ideals prove unrealistic and result in disillusionment. Also, some ideals yield to other interests or are abandoned for lack of energy and time (recall our earlier statement regarding the need for attention and the limited nature of psychic energy). A good example of this evolving process of idealization is the adolescent's changing ideas about future career choices.

Nonetheless, the process of investing in ideals is inherently value laden due to the normative nature of ego idealizations. That is, the working of the ego ideal not only offers aspiration for the adolescent's quest, it also shapes the adolescent's vision of the future through eliciting core interests and authentic expressions of adolescent desires. In other words, the ego ideal serves to invite what we might term *metaquestions*. A metaquestion moves beyond isolated incidents and narrow focus; it is an overarching question that provides direction and interdependence with the very fabric of the adolescent's life. Questions that the ego ideal elicits are, What do I dream for? What am I to become? In what should I invest my life? Such questions are inherently value laden. It is only with adolescence, particularly the middle and late adolescent years, that such questions can be addressed. Due to the developmental need for the adolescent to find meaning and to incorporate more meaningful ideals and maturing life projects, the wise adult (whose own relationship with the adolescent, as we saw in chapter 2, is a significant presence for creating the climate for reflecting on such questions) serves as a model of how one can address such questions.

By late adolescence, idealizations are transformed into more mature and lasting efforts, such as investment in a career and the sustained commitment of enduring and mutually supportive relationships. In this ongoing experience of relationship building, the adolescent encounters a wide variety of experiences that foster joy, disappointment, and sorrow, as well as deepening self-knowledge and intimacy. All in all, these experiences are a valuable source for clarifying values and personal goals. In the process of forming deepening relationships and engaging in more meaningful ventures, the adolescent comes to discover his or her capacity for commitment to personal values and life goals. These sustained commitments, in turn, express the adolescent's deepest ideals inasmuch as they embody the values that reflect the adolescent's core sense of self.

Along this aspirational path, there also evolves a more realistic notion of the ideal as well as a deepening disclosure of what this ideal represents in terms of one's core sense of value. Indeed, the values to which one pledges oneself become defining features for adulthood.

The malfunctioning of the ego ideal, on the other hand, leads to the formulation of unrealistic aspirations. At times, some adolescents invest in life projects or idealize others in ways that create unacceptable expectations. As a consequence, these adolescents are openly critical and never satisfied. Their demands are continually frustrated and they experience constant dissatisfaction with themselves, those around them, and their environment. Another source of ego-ideal distress is the adolescent who invests in the self as the primary source of idealization. Although it is quite natural for adolescents to invest psychologically in their own selves and display what might be termed a tolerable level of egotism or narcissism, some adolescents are so invested in their own selves that they create for themselves a narcissistic shield that prevents healthy attachment and maturing life projects. From a psychological perspective, both of these examples reflect more serious psychological issues and often require professional intervention.

Self-esteem

When the ego ideal is functioning adequately, the child or adolescent develops an adequate sense of self-satisfaction. We define self-esteem as a felt sense of inner pride in the self's ability to obtain an increasing sense of personal satisfaction. Ultimately, it reflects the self as valued, not only for what it does, but simply for what it *is*. Self-esteem hinges on adequate parental care. The infant's attachment with the parent provides a felt sense of security and gratification and leads to a feeling of the self as "good." This valuation of the self as good furnishes a child with the psychological resources to sustain the sorrows, disappointments, and failures that are threaded through development.

At the same time, a second source of self-esteem arises with the child's active mastery of the environment. The infant, for example, who gradually acquires muscle coordination becomes capable of movement and can obtain immediate goals. As more and more developmental tasks are mastered, the child experiences a feeling of self-worth and the capacity to master his or her environment.

Ideally, childhood development is marked by increasing self-worth and ongoing mastery of tasks. With the advent of adolescence, however, the child's self-esteem is once again threatened. This threat to self-esteem originates in psychological changes and a rupture in the adolescent's self-continuity. That is, adolescence represents a period of questioning and reevaluation of self. Often an increasingly introspective self-examination arises with biological changes, more sophisticated thinking (leading inevitably to personal doubt and questioning), and the experience of more deeply felt emotions. All in all, the adolescent is thrust into a spotlight whereby essential questions of self-worth emerge as significant. Furthermore, this radical questioning of self is encouraged by the expectations of society that slowly but inexorably require the adolescent to assess and acquire appropriate behaviors and attitudes in preparation for adult responsibility.

Adolescents unable to achieve success and adequate mastery of their environment are subject to feelings of worthlessness and self-doubt. Moreover, some adolescents can develop a profound sense of personal inadequacy, which leads to a precarious tentativeness regarding their own commitments. Equally important, many adolescents, burdened by their self-doubt, often resort to regressive forms of behavior in order to cope with the pressures of daily life and the personal inadequacy they feel.

The significance of self-esteem for a psychology of conscience arises from two sources. The first is the sense of attachment. The second is the capacity for self-honesty.

In essence, self-esteem exists because one feels valued. This valuation of self, as noted above, arises originally from the felt sense of soothing and positive feelings emanating from the parent-child bond. This initial bonding is like a microcosm of the effects that transpire from later attachments. It is important to underscore the role of attachment in self-esteem. The self exists within relationship. This relationship resides first with parental figures and is later expanded to include siblings, extended family, and peer relationships. Yet attachment is more than interpersonal relationships, it includes bonding to social entities, such as schools, clubs, ethnic groups, neighborhood, and nation. In other words, there exists a social dimension to attachment that goes beyond the interpersonal. The product of the self's evolving consolidation of self-esteem is the felt sense of belonging and the experience of being valued as a member of a group, along with pride for and in the group. The consequences of safe attachment help to secure one's sense of value and foster self-identity that leads in turn to greater appropriation of the values that reflect one's identity.

The second critical role for self-esteem arises from its role in insuring self-honesty. Unless one feels an adequate sense of "goodness" it becomes difficult to engage in healthy self-reflection. Deficiency in self-esteem produces limited and guarded self-reflection, denial, or ego inflation, characterized by the seeking of compensating behaviors to support inadequate self-esteem. In other words, unless the self has a felt sense of its own goodness, it cowers at the possibility of serious self-examination. Obviously, feelings of self-esteem are critical for moral maturity inasmuch as they allow for personal responsibility and engender the psychic strength needed for challenging and even prophetic witness to the Gospel.

Teleology

Conscience, as we noted at the beginning of this chapter, functions in a deliberative and reflective way. This functioning reflects the teleological dimension of conscience. I would place the moral reasoning of Kohlberg under this dimension. Kohlberg's dilemmas evoke responses that show one's "reasons" for a moral behavior. It is the teleological thrust of conscience to render such reasons interpretable and compelling. The teleological nature of conscience, likewise, serves the purpose of self-critique. This capacity for self-examination blends inextricably with the acceptance of personal responsibility for one's actions. In turn, acknowledging personal responsibility is wedded to the awareness of one's capacity for choice. (By the time the child is four, he or she is aware there exists some possibility for choice.[24])

Unfortunately, the discipline of psychology has minimized the roles of personal responsibility and free will. Most psychologists prefer a mechanistic and materialistic view of human functioning. Nevertheless, psychologists themselves are beginning to challenge this narrow view of human nature. Recent writing in psychology has focused on values and the freedom humans exercise when making their moral decisions.

Psychologist Joseph Rychlak is one of the most prominent proponents of the role of free will and human responsibility in human decision making. Rychlak has taken a teleological (telic) view of human nature, which, he notes, undergirds the human experience of freedom. In essence, psychology has been preoccupied with how humans respond. What is important, however, is not responding to something but responding "for the sake of" something. That "for the sake of which" we respond gives purpose and meaning to our actions. This view of human nature is known as teleology (telic). A telic view of human nature states that human action is based upon "purposive meanings—and therefore directed to some intended end."[25] That is, one provides intentionality for his or her actions. For example, a door is simply a door; it is the human who gives purposeful meaning to the door's reality through his or her intention to open or shut the door. According to Rychlak, humans do not simply respond to stimuli; rather, they respond in telic ways. They give meaning to their overt responses. For example, one could decide to drive a car. A behaviorist would speak of the numerous stimuli and responses that lead to one's getting into the car and driving away. A telic interpretation of this account would proceed differently. A telic interpretation would focus on the recognition of the car, the walk through the driveway to the car, and the judgment to put these mental events (as well as others) together. In other words, there is a mental act which logically precedes the response of driving away, it is that "for the sake of which I do something"— the human judgment that one chooses to take a drive in the car. Furthermore, as the self affirms the judgment to drive the car, it always has the option to do the opposite. Humans, in effect, are capable of dialectic reasoning and can choose the opposite of their present action. At any point, for example, one could choose not to drive the car. One could always make a judgment contrary to what one originally chooses. Rychlak also notes that every human being is by nature required to "take a position on" the passing scenes of his or her life, and therefore choice or decision is *always* involved in this process even when this selective process is personally unnoticed.

The role of personal responsibility comes into play when a human being realizes the need to affirm the grounds "for the sake of which" he or she does something. For example, we might have grown accustomed out of habit to spend a few minutes of each day in prayer. At some point this was a conscious decision on our part, though our original decision is now distant from our consciousness. However, if over a few days we are pressed for time and give up our time for prayer, we are soon forced consciously to make a decision as to whether we are going to honor our original decision to pray. In other words, we must make a decision and choose "that for the sake of which" we pray or do not pray. Inevitably, we are forced to take a position on our prayer life and examine the true rationale for our decision to continue to pray or not to pray. To be sure, "the realities of life" might limit what we might actually be able to choose. Yet, every person is endowed with the capacity to affirm the sake for which he or she chooses a certain action. Every person can at some point examine the premises that form the basis for why he or she does something. "When we come right down to it, this something involves a close examination of the grounding assumptions, beliefs, values, etc., which premise behavior."[26] In other words, each person invariably must examine the fundamental orientation to value that guides his or her own life. It is through this process of self-examination that we take personal responsibility for our lives.

The role of intentionality is vital for the development of the adolescent's moral self. In essence, the adolescent must face directly the intentional nature of his or her life and develop guides to consistent and sustained behavior that are value laden. Increasingly, the adolescent is expected to provide reasons for his or her behavior and be able at the same time to express the values that guide his or her life. Erikson has noted that the adolescent who lacks purpose is relegated to a diffuse state, and subject to shifting and limited goals and meaningless activities and pursuits.

The adolescent is pressed to respond to significant questions such as: What is the meaning of my life? How am I taking responsibility for this meaning? What are my deepest desires? What are my goals? The pressing need to respond to such questions compels the adolescent to search for a life direction that is grounded in purposeful meaning and life values.

In describing the role of the mental health expert, psychoanalyst Robert Atkinson notes that the analyst can assist the adolescent by serving as a guide in helping the adolescent form a purposeful view of life. He states that adolescent intentions, ultimately, must reside in

> something they choose to believe in. They set their sights, though unconsciously at first, on the goals and ideals passed on to them by their parents. Their programmed self succeeds in becoming the executor of the goals, purposes, and ambitions that they had at some point made their own. Perhaps, then, a corollary trademark of the analyst might be to help the adolescent bring about from the plurality of options being faced a clearly focused sense of purpose or to help the adolescent begin to recognize a pattern that will point to the inner connection of parts to the whole of life that is unfolding, as this sense of purpose can become a pivotal component of well-being and integrity in later life.[27]

This description aptly serves the pastoral minister who is attempting to aid the adolescent in taking responsibility for his or her actions. The pastoral minister becomes a ready resource for feedback and challenge, thereby helping the adolescent to crystallize a sense of purpose through the responsible use of his or her freedom.

Universality: The Key to Maturity in Conscience Functioning

So far we have set forth the essential dimensions of a psychology of conscience. We have argued that it is attention to this "nature" of conscience that sustains, through the infusion of God's self-communicating presence, the Christian notion of conscience that we have defined as conscience of other-centered value. Having explored the nature of conscience, we now turn to the defining feature that characterizes conscience. In other words, given that this psychological foundation exists, what is the essential moral feature of such psychological functioning? What is the result of this maturing integration of the seven dimensions discussed above? The central and essential thrust of a maturely functioning conscience is its capacity for *universality*. Within the context of a psychology of conscience, we mean the application of moral principles to self and others. Indeed, the problem of conscience is essentially accepting that one's own self is subject to the same moral commands that one uses to judge others.

The essential moral challenge facing each person is the inability to apply moral principles to the self. That is, individuals are more prone to apply moral principles to others while exempting themselves from such scrutiny. Thus, a woman might be overly critical of her friend, yet fail to realize that she, too, is guilty of similar misdeeds. A husband can find shortcomings in his wife, while ignoring his own contribution to marital discord. Although we focus here on individuals, it is true that institutions are also culpable. Thus in an election year a political party's platform might readily criticize the other party, yet shy away from a searching and critical examination of its own record. Nations are all too willing to point out the problems of other nations while ignoring their own shortcomings. Conscience remains the single guiding force that pricks the deceit and self-deception that afflicts our moral lives. Conscience, in other words, is the sole mechanism for making moral principles applicable to our own situation. From conscience emerges our capacity for self-criticism.

How might these psychological dimensions of conscience act to support the capacity for self-criticism? An excellent way to explore this process is to examine the story of David and Bathsheba in the eleventh chapter of the Second Book of Samuel. The story's "moral" is contained in chapter 12, when the prophet Nathan confronts David and his sin.[28]

The story is well known. David remains in Jerusalem while his army is locked in bloody conflict. One night, while on his balcony, he notices a woman (Bathsheba) for whom he lusts. David has relations with Bathsheba while her husband, Uriah, an armor bearer, is away doing battle with the enemies of Israel. A short time after their sexual tryst, Bathsheba sends word that she is pregnant. In order to cover up his sin, David sends for Uriah the Hittite and under the pretext of having him report on the military situation, he encourages him to spend time with Bathsheba and to rest after his military exploits. Uriah refuses the opportunity to be with Bathsheba in order to be in solidarity with his battle-weary comrades in the field. David, frustrated that his plan did not work, orders the commanding officer to place Uriah in a position in the battle where his life will be in danger. David's wish comes true when he receives a report that Uriah was killed in battle. Subsequently, after a period of mourning, Bathsheba is taken into David's house.

As is typical of Old Testament prophets, Nathan appears in the story as the voice of Yahweh. In order to impress upon David the gravity of his sin, Nathan shares with the king a poignant story of a poor man who had a little lamb. The poor man loved the lamb and, indeed, "she was like a daughter to him" (2 Sam. 12:3). One day a wealthy neighbor took the poor man's lamb and slaughtered it in order to feed it to a guest. David is outraged by such a callous act and vows, "as the Lord lives, the man who has done this merits death. He shall restore the ewe lamb fourfold because he has done this and has had no pity" (2 Sam. 12:5–6). At this point, Nathan confronts David with the awful truth—"You are the man!"—and proceeds to admonish David for his treacherous deed. Nathan's revelation of the truth leads David to remorse as he realizes his heinous act.

On the surface, this story appears clear-cut. Yet, the real tragedy of the story is not David's hypocrisy in his all-too-eager willingness to punish the rich man. The real tragedy of David is his inability to apply moral principles to himself:

> often when that text is discussed, one hears a good deal about David's hypocrisy having been finally unmasked. But that is a poor analysis, for David's conduct in the case is not significantly hypocritical. His moral judgment of the fictitious case was perfectly sincere, and his indignation was authentically moral. The standard he judged by was really and deeply his own. The irony of the tale is not its contrasting of real with pretended principles, but its contrasting of principled objectivity with unprincipled subjectivity.[29]

David no doubt was conversant with moral principles and he decided them rightly in the case presented by Nathan. His moral failure was his inability to apply these same principles to himself. As moralist James Gaffney asserts,

> What has always been thought to distinguish persons of deep moral integrity is an interior component of themselves that is always found ready, when the time comes, to say to them in effect what Nathan said to David, "You are the man," requiring them to play their own game and keep their own score by the same rules they apply to others. They can be equipped with such rules by normative ethics. But only by conscience can they be brought to apply rules to themselves.[30]

David's failure symbolizes the failure of every person. All too often we are knowledgeable regarding moral principles and smoothly (indeed, at times effortlessly!) apply them to others, yet remain elusively pliant when there is need to subject ourselves to these same principles.

Utilizing the dimensions of a psychology of conscience, we might briefly sketch and seek to understand David's failing. One might fault David's attention. It is unclear why he stayed back while his troops were engaged in battle, though it is not necessary that the king always accompany his troops. We know nothing of David's attentional focus, though we do know that he was attracted to Bathsheba. Unfortunately, we are not told the viewpoint of the woman. Nathan's moral admonitions are limited in this respect for he fails to include the feelings, thoughts, and viewpoint of Uriah's wife. In any case, we do know that David desired Bathsheba and a considerable degree of psychic energy must have been involved in this attraction as well as the plan to manipulate and then kill Bathsheba's husband. We might speculate that this channeling of psychic energy eclipsed other endeavors which could serve to thwart his amorous wishes and wicked designs.

Though David showed neither sensitivity nor compassion toward Uriah, he was not devoid of empathy. For one, when asked to judge the account given him by Nathan he readily expressed moral outrage at the treatment of the poor man and most likely empathized with his plight. Yet, the key issue here is the limit of David's empathy; as noted, he was unable to empathize with Uriah, thereby shutting off conscience's sensitivity. What this teaches us is the power of empathy as a moral catalyst, yet it also allows us to see its limits.

David appeared to experience little guilt until confronted by Nathan; then he showed deep remorse for his sin. We might speculate that if he had lacked self-esteem he would have sought an excuse for his action; lacking self-esteem, he would have been unable to face his guilt. Yet, David's moral frailty was starkly exposed by his blindness to the moral gravity of his actions. In the midst of his moral error, his own self-esteem was sufficiently threatened so as to preclude his acknowledging his moral failure.

The role of David's ideals is also central to understanding the psychological dynamics of his conscience. One could conclude that David possessed ideals he lived by. Certainly his own experience of the Lord's care of him was pivotal for his life (for example, Yahweh's protection of him during his estrangement from Saul). Yet, his ideals remained incomplete. His own life project at some level lacked a depth that would inspire him to live according to Yahweh's law. There existed insufficient psychic investment in the role of being a servant of the Lord. Stated another way, the image and ideal of himself as king over the people he governed failed to shape some aspect of his life. That ideal which calls forth an inner integrity and self-sacrifice was either compartmentalized within him or shielded by other factors. David, essentially, was engaged in self-deception. He was caught in his own lie, a lie to himself. Yet, he was able to take personal responsibility for himself when confronted with his sin. His inner image of self, his valued ideal, was capable of discerning the truth when challenged. Not surprisingly, David most likely had deep respect for the prophetic tradition, hence his ability to hear Nathan's challenge (recall that one characteristic of conscience is its capacity for openness).

The essence of David's failure of conscience was, I suspect, his use of psychological defenses, especially his capacity for rationalization and minimalization. Naturally, we have no way of knowing his reasoning. Perhaps the seductive enchantment of power allowed him at some level to believe himself immune to the Lord's command (one is reminded here of Lord Acton's famous comment that power corrupts and absolute power corrupts absolutely). It might have been that he had grown so accustomed to the ravages of war and violence that Uriah's death was just one more death he could minimalize and rationalize away. David's psychological defenses effectively shielded him from the self-honesty one would expect of the Lord's servant. David did not abrogate his conscience, but he did, it appears, compromise it for personal convenience.

Of course the observations given above are conjecture. We have no way of proving what was actually occurring psychologically within David. Even more importantly, we are not attempting to psychologize away David's sin. Fundamentally, David turned from the Lord because of his selfish desires and personal greed. Yet, this turning from the Lord's ways necessitated not only his rejection of the Lord, but also the activating psychological dynamics which colluded to bring about his refusal.

David's story is attractive because it is our story, too. The psychology of David is our psychology. It is the psychology of inadequate or flawed ideals. It is the experience of shielding ourselves through self-deceptions. David's refusal to take responsibility all too often mirrors our own refusal to be accountable for our lives. Guilt is nowhere to be found as David plots his machinations; like David, we are all too willing to compartmentalize the experiences of guilt that could galvanize our sensitivities.

As noted above, the adolescent is vulnerable to many of the shortcomings that compromised David. The fragile nature of adolescent conscience formation leaves the young person easily exposed to the vagaries and deceptions of this period. Attentional deficits and the wasteful expenditure of psychic energy often expose adolescents to temptation or close them off from the maturing experience that fosters self-insight and self-honesty. Adolescent "hypocrisy" is often in evidence as the young person, unsure of self, externalizes blame or rationalizes his or her own faults. Perplexed by their own emotions, adolescents can overempathize or erratically display both compassion and distance toward others. Many adolescents are crippled by superego guilt and suffer from inadequate self-esteem. In addition, many adolescents might not have hopes and dreams that are constructive, nor are they fashioning a personal philosophy or ethical code that energizes and expands their conscience. In such ways they limit the sensitivity and critical reflection that nurtures their moral lives.

One final point needs mentioning. Having examined the weaknesses of the adolescent moral self, we turn to the integration of the seven psychological dimensions. I do not view the psychological functioning of conscience as taking place in a linear fashion. In other words, the dimensions of conscience as I have outlined them do not occur one after the other. (One does not first focus attention on something and then activate psychological defenses and after their activation begin to empathize, and so on.)

Rather, I view the psychological functioning of conscience as a tapestry in which each color of thread—each dimension—intersects with every other color. No color stands alone, and each color enhances the overall configuration (symbolized as the functioning of conscience). It is the blending of the colors that gives the tapestry its beauty and appeal. Likewise, it is the interactional effect of each dimension upon the others that provides for the integration and maturity of conscience, thereby sustaining self-reflection and the capacity for self-examination.

The effective use of psychic energy broadens conscience and encourages mature defensive functioning. Attention to developmental tasks fosters empathic reactions and allows for appropriate experiences of guilt. Further, self-esteem is enhanced and constructive ideals are maintained and developed. Finally, responsible use of one's freedom and a developing life plan animates one's future goals. The interactional effect of each dimension strengthens the overall thrust of conscience as other-centered.

An outline of this interactional effect of conscience's seven psychological dimensions is given in figure 1. The arrows signify each dimension's interaction with every other dimension. The single arrows reflect the influence that each dimension has on conscience as the source of other-centered value. The box in which the dimensions are enclosed represents the supporting environment that nourishes the development of each dimension. This rectangle reflects such realities as the quality of family life, faith community, and relationship formations. The dimensions both individually and as an interactional process, are dependent upon the support received from the enclosure within the rectangle. Integral to this whole endeavor is the experience of God's self-communicating presence, which sustains the entire process.

As we have discussed, each dimension of conscience has unique characteristics that signify healthy and unhealthy growth dynamics. Naturally, such characteristics impact on adolescent

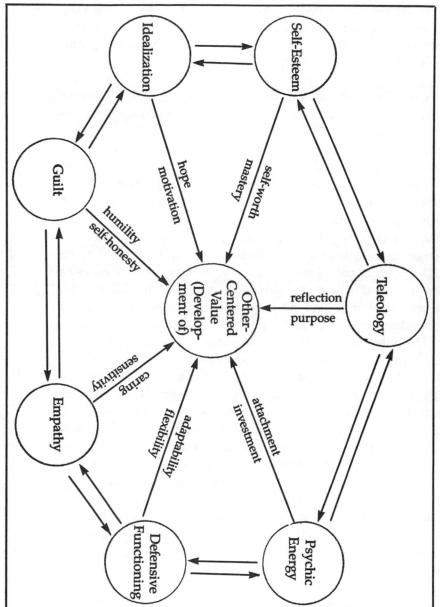

FIGURE 1

THE DYNAMIC FUNCTIONING OF CONSCIENCE AS OTHER-CENTERED VALUE

O = psychological reality

☐ = sustaining, supporting environment

➤ = some of the dimensional features which sustain growth of other-centered value

FIGURE 2

SOME DEVELOPMENTAL FEATURES OF CONSCIENCE FORMATION

Adolescence ——— ——— ——— ——> Adulthood

Dimension	Polarities (Some Examples)	Some Adult Characteristics
Psychic Energy	Adaptive (healthy attachment, openness, mastery of developmental tasks)	Flexibility, generative
	Nonadaptive (fixations, dissipates energy)	Unfocused, distracted, regressive
Defensive Functioning	Mature (healthy adaptive functioning)	Adaptable, realistic
	Immature (inability to cope with stress and conflicts, unrealistic view of self and world)	Rigid, erratic, immature
Empathy	Care (sensitivity, compassion)	Compassionate, caring life stance
	Insensitive (insensitivity, compulsive care giving, overempathizing)	Isolated, insensitive, clinging
Guilt	Moral (humility, increasing self-honesty)	Integrity, humble stance
	Superego (poor self-image, self-doubt, worry)	Intropunitive, tension, doubt, rigid
Idealization	Hope (realistic optimism, goal seeking, ideals to live by)	Optimism, hopefulness, self-satisfaction
	Overidealizing (unrealistic aspiration, egotistical, critical)	Chronic dissatisfaction with self and others
Self-esteem	Inner Goodness (realistic self-worth, self-honesty)	Self-confidence, gratefulness
	Inadequacy (inferiority, overcompensating)	Pervasive feelings of inadequacy
Teleology	Purposeful (responsible, reflective)	Mature moral reasoning
	Diffuse (unable to take responsibility, inability to articulate moral stance)	Lack of reflective value system

velopment and have consequences for adult functioning. The chart in figure 2 details, from a developmental perspective, the effect of each dimension.

The adult pastoral minister who works with youth needs to address these dimensions of conscience. It is likely that at particular moments in the adolescent's life, one or more of these dimensions will profit from reflective focus and pastoral interventions that are supportive, challenging, or insight oriented. When we discussed the story of David, we noted Nathan's crucial role in addressing the laxity of David's conscience. Nathan symbolizes two realities. First, the prophet represents the openness every person must have toward life in order continually to seek the truth and be challenged. David's willingness to hear Nathan, to ponder his words, and to admit his sin reflects the ever-present need for exposing conscience to challenge and truth. This continual exposure to life and its mystery animates the self-reflective nature of conscience, nourishing its capacity to examine critically the self's attitudes and behaviors.

The second significance of Nathan resides, simply, in his presence. Our discussion has shown that conscience is intimately linked to the relational ties that bond people to one another. Initially, these are the significant ties of parental attachment, but they soon branch out to include other adults, friends, and peers. By adolescence they embrace significant adults who have become models and guiding influences for later development. As such, the adult is offered a critical role in helping to form the conscience of youth. One can even view the adult's presence as an intrusive one; most certainly, Nathan intruded forcefully into the consciousness of David. We might envision the pastoral role of the adult as a gentle yet intruding presence that seeks to further critical self-reflection by encouraging the adolescent to reflect critically on his or her life. The thrust of the adult's efforts, in other words, is that of loving intrusion.

Regardless of whether the adult's role is that of counselor, teacher, or pastoral minister, there are critical aspects of each dimension that need to be explored. Below are a list of questions the adult might use as a guide when reflecting with the adolescent on each of the dimensions of conscience we have examined. Pastoral sensitivity (not to mention time restraints) prevent any extended discussion of all dimensions with the adolescent during any one (or even several) pastoral encounter(s). Focusing on one or two areas in any discussion would be the norm. These questions might also form the basis for group and class discussions.

Adaptive Psychic Energy

What experiences does the adolescent most attend to?

What does the adolescent most focus on?

How do you describe the "quality" of the adolescent's attention?

To what does the adolescent give priority in his or her life?

What are the adolescent's goals? Does he or she deem goals as important?

Do the adolescent's investments of time and energy lead to reflection on personal values?

Defensive Functioning

Does the adolescent blame others for his or her faults?

Is there a tendency for this adolescent to rationalize? To what extent?

Does the adolescent downplay his or her need to take personal responsibility?

Does the adolescent compartmentalize various areas of his or her life and refuse to look at areas in which there is need for self-evaluation (e.g., sexuality, home life, school).

In what ways does the adolescent stereotype others and refuse to see and accept differences among others?

Does the adolescent have a tendency to be overly preoccupied or absorbed in some projects? Do some investments of the adolescent's time and energy shield him or her from facing other issues in his or her life?

To what extent can the adolescent "control" his or her impulses?

How aware is the adolescent of his or her immature ways of coping with personal insecurities and the avoidance of personal responsibility?

In what ways does this adolescent resolve personal conflicts and internal tensions?

Does the adolescent have opportunities to be creative?

How does the adolescent care for others? What is the "quality" of this care? Is there a compulsive nature to his or her care?

Is the adolescent capable of ongoing commitments? How honest is the adolescent about his or her commitments? Are some commitments overly rigid? Is the adolescent open to new possibilities and altering some commitments if necessary? What "criteria" does the adolescent utilize when evaluating his or her commitments?

How does the adolescent use humor? Does it "build up" others?

Empathy

How does the adolescent show sensitivity to others?

What is the adolescent's capacity for empathizing with others?

Does the adolescent overempathize?

How does the adolescent respond to his or her empathic stirrings?

Does the adolescent have appropriate channels for expressing his or her empathic feelings?

How does the adolescent respond to the distress of others?

Are there instances in which the adolescent refuses to acknowledge (deny) his or her empathic feelings?

Can the adolescent empathize and still keep a healthy distance (maintain ego boundaries and not overidentify)?

Can the adolescent articulate and explore the values he or she associates with empathic experiences that he or she experiences?

Guilt

What in this adolescent's life leads him or her to experience guilt?

In what ways does the adolescent deny guilt?

Do experiences of guilt burden this adolescent (influence his or her self-esteem and sense of "inner goodness")?

What is the quality of "humility" and "sense of forgiveness" associated with this adolescent's guilt feelings?

Idealization

What are this adolescent's dreams, hopes, desires?

Is this adolescent a "hopeful" person?

What experiences give this adolescent a sense of pride?

What is this adolescent's view of his or her future?

What values are reflected by the adolescent in the four questions listed above?

Does this adolescent overidealize?

Are there areas in his or her life where there never seems to be a sense of satisfaction?

Self-Esteem

What attachments serve as embodiments for this adolescent's ideals (for example, family, peer group, faith community, ethnic group)?

Does the adolescent recognize the association between his values and the numerous influences that have formed his attitudes and perspectives?

What are the sources of this adolescent's self-esteem?

To what extent is this adolescent unable to accept various aspects of his or her self (e.g., physical characteristics, limits to talents, family relationship)? How does this lack of self-acceptance affect this adolescent's life?

Teleology

To what extent can this adolescent take personal responsibility for his or her behavior?

Can the adolescent articulate reasons "why" certain behaviors or attitudes endure?

Can the adolescent identify what influences him or her to engage in certain behaviors?

Does this adolescent show the motivation and capacity to reflect critically on his or her life?

The Phenomenal Reality of Value

Two psychological realities must be addressed in order to grasp more completely the adolescent's moral experience. The first is the blending of normal maturational processes (psychological growth) with the growing experience of value in the adolescent's life. The second reality is the ongoing choice of value in the concrete situations of everyday life. We term the former the experience of *morally felt foundations* whereas the latter is expressed through *moral identity*. It is helpful to distinguish between these two realities. For example, I can have a felt sense of myself as honest. This awareness is the experience of my life—the gradual, habitual experience of myself in everyday life. However, there exist meaningful moments where, upon reflection, I come to define myself as a person who is honest. In other words, at some point I "own" this honesty through dealing with temptation or a challenge that tests my honesty. I come to realize that honesty is part of my core definition of self. In other words, to reflect upon myself is to state that this honesty is central and significant to who I am. In effect, it is part of my self-definition. The adolescent experiences these two realities. Through childhood he or she is exposed to and experiences a felt sense of value, yet this value is continually tested through either developmental changes or life experience. At various points in the adolescent years, however, the young person must choose to accept some values as central for a definition of self.

Morally Felt Foundations

The scene is typical: Jim, an eighteen-year-old high school senior, has been rejected by his girlfriend. A relationship that only six months ago was intense and seemed permanent, is now ruptured by misunderstanding. Unable to accept the reality of this broken relationship, Jim retreats into himself and, although still involved in school activities, his feelings are wounded and his ability to reach out to peers is lessened. This passive psychological state is only one of several defensive strategies that Jim could employ. For example, some adolescents might become hostile and lash out verbally at the concern shown by well-intentioned friends. Others blindly invest themselves in new projects or relationships in order to ease their hurt. Still others simply deny the whole experience and attempt to act as if life was going on "as usual." The rupturing of relationships or the termination of commitments occupies an important role in the psychological development of the adolescent. Through experiences such as disappointments youth come to understand the scope and intensity of their emotional needs and personal desires.

Yet Jim's story characterizes one of the central difficulties in the human quest to develop a moral self. The dilemma is this: Every person is in need of psychically rooted and enduring attachments. These experiences allow one to pledge the self to future growth. They make possible future ventures because one is presently rooted in a felt security that encourages future exploration. It is this subjective experience of psychic investment and attachment that ushers in a growing understanding of personal value. What is prized and cherished in one's deepest self is brought to the forefront by the psychic rootedness present in one's life. An important relationship or a cause to which one has devoted considerable time and energy interweaves with growing self-knowledge. The result is a deepening self-disclosure of value and life meaning. This psychic attachment coupled with growing self-awareness of value forms the basis for what I term morally felt foundations.

One's openness to life allows for the greater discovery of value. The ongoing experience of personal self-discovery and value disclosure reflects the radical openness to life to which every Christian is called. In short, "finding God" (which from the Christian perspective we propose is the integration of the entire experience of one's personal reality to grace—one's thoughts, feelings, intuitions) reflects the impulse of our self-transcending nature to respond charitably in self-sacrificing and caring ways toward others. Within this process of value discovery, God does not "tell me" what I should do. Rather, what God's communicating presence does do is open up horizons for my freedom in order that I may freely choose in the decisions of my life to model my life after the life, death, and resurrection of Jesus.

In this context, morally felt foundations serve as the psychological grounding for my freedom. They express my striving for self-sacrifice and fidelity and sustain the hope to which I am called (1 Pet. 3:15). In essence, to "have value" is to experience the presence of value in the ongoing development of my life. An example is helpful. An adult might have a career from which she derives an immense amount of self-satisfaction and gratification. Her work sustains her self-identity and is fulfilling. Over the years her work has offered her the opportunity to reflect on her self-knowledge and experience a number of enduring relationships. The psychic attachment she has invested in her career as well as the numerous experiences that have enhanced her life have fostered a growing psychic stability (strength of self-knowledge, self-esteem, self-identity) and numerous opportunities to express her values. Her experience of value is, hopefully, expressed through the evolution of life's decisions modeled after Christian values.

The psychic rootedness of value that we offer for growth must continually confront the demands and limits of everyday reality. Personal limitations and economic realities, for example, might shape the type of morally felt foundations one might experience. Moreover, at times these foundations might be eclipsed by personal loss or emotional conflict.

Ideally, in the mature adult there exists a plentiful admixture of these foundations. The adult has available several nurturing relationships (with spouse or close friends) that have born the test of time. In addition there is a vocational commitment that nourishes the interests, goals, and desires of the adult and is an avenue for reflection about who he or she truly is. Finally, there might be hobbies or other projects in which the adult invests time and energy, thus profiting from greater self-insight and the testing of undiscovered sides of the self; furthermore, these added interests integrate and sharpen value commitments in various areas of daily life. Each of these experiences points to a permanency and articulated value that is continually integrated into one's own life. Equally important, the learning, insight, and self-knowledge that arise from these morally felt foundations enable one to embrace what is transcendently noble in human experience: truth, fidelity, knowledge, and self-sacrifice.

It is within this framework that the frailty accompanying the adolescent's moral quest must be understood. In essence, high school and college undergraduates lack, to various degrees, the very rooted experiences so necessary for the emergence of a personal sense of value permanency. That is, the adolescent is vulnerable to the pressing demands of identity and intimacy. He or she, likewise, must sort out numerous vocational choices as well as innumerable experiences that help to fashion and portray who "I really am." The blending of these experiences leads the young person on a gradual discovery of what is noble and good within human experience. Yet, it is a search the adolescent treads cautiously. At first, there appears a tentativeness which can be paralyzing. With time, most young people begin to make initial commitments. A first love, the excitement over finding a friend, or the discovery of a career possibility that "fits," enables the adolescent to acquire knowledge of the self as well as explore the values these experiences elicit. Unfortunately, this road of initial psychic investments is fraught with other experiences, too. Fondness for another (as Jim discovered) is often fleeting and termination is an all-too-real possibility. Friends move away or have misunderstandings. Vocational interests wax and wane within the evolving process of self-discovery. The vicissitudes of changing desires, and the sometimes painful realization of limited talents, are added factors. Even the support of family can be eclipsed by the urgent need to distance oneself from family ties in order to accede to the ever present urgency to establish self-identity.

In sum, this relentless lack of permanency (enduring psychic attachment) leaves the adolescent in a state of drift. The constant flux of unrealized commitments subject many youth to psychic drift. As a consequence, many young people search for those experiences that add some dimension of meaning to their lives. For some adolescents this search is fraught with crisis.

In an earlier chapter we noted that one of the most crucial priorities for pastoral ministry and religious education is the encouragement of morally felt foundations in the ongoing experiences of youth. In order to explore the basis for these morally felt foundations, we need to delineate the moral source for such experience.

Basis for Moral Foundations

Matthew's Gospel contains one of the most haunting questions in Scripture. In chapter 16 Jesus arrives at Caesarea Philippi and asks, "who do you say that I am?" The question is simple; yet for each of us the answer we give is profound. Jesus does not ask about one's attitudes or ideas. He does not suggest that we theologize or produce some abstract or highly discursive prose. Furthermore, he does not ask the question of a well-financed or highly educated group of scholars. The question is simple, direct, and, above all, personal. Within the depths of one's heart the Lord poses this most fundamental of questions. He beckons from each person a response that is genuine. No one else can answer this question for another; it

113

is inescapable. It is the deepest self that the Lord calls forth to answer this question. As Pierre Ganne notes:

> when it comes to answering the question which Christ directs to us personally, no other person or thing can answer in our name. Neither philosophy nor science, nor theology, not even the Church, whose role is certainly not to substitute for the irreplaceable act of personal faith.[31]

Yet how is such a question best answered? One could respond with "the Christ" or "the Savior" but perhaps these replies are simply the repetitive products of narrow intellectual reflection. This does not mean that such answers are not true, yet they can often lack the sustained and responsible reflection that such a question deserves.

The real response to Jesus' question comes through one's openness to the mystery of life. This openness involves the investing of one's psyche in commitments that at their deepest level yield the transcendent values which proclaim the life of Jesus as well as who we are called to be (Gal. 2:20). To answer this question means to invest the self more deeply in meaningful relational encounters that are oriented to fidelity, growth, and other-centeredness. Moreover, it includes a commitment to vocational aspirations and those experiences which tap into the darkness, the unexplored and underdeveloped sides of one's life. It is the blending of psychic energy, sustained attachment, and the growing realization of value that answers Jesus' question. Through this interweaving one gradually comes to realize that the psychic rootedness in one's life experience is value laden. These experiences are morally felt foundations. They are the psychological realities of life that, when identified through their values, allow one increasingly to venture forth and respond to the Gospel's call. These foundations serve as steppingstones to a deeper exploration of the Lord's invitation to follow him. These foundations orient experience to deepening levels of valued meaning. As these morally felt foundations are experienced, one becomes more capable of responding to Jesus' question. The answer to his question is the discovery of value realized through one's openness to life. Experiencing life, moreover, through a growing acceptance of God's self-communicating presence draws forth ever deepening levels of humility, forgiveness, honesty, and commitment.

Moral Identity

In reviewing the experience of morally felt foundations, we come to see the adolescent as capable of a growing awareness of value in his or her life. In turn, to realize value is to ask, "What ought I to do?" Values represent normative concerns, they point to some deeply held belief that is pivotal for one's self-definition, and they orient one to a specific course of action. As noted above, they contain a sense of "oughtness," of that which must be done. Still, the question must be asked as to "why" the adolescent might respond in a caring and loving way: in other words, even though the adolescent is oriented to values that are other-centered and altruistic, he or she does not necessarily have to choose such values. In this regard, one is reminded of the person who espouses altruism but who, when confronted with an actual situation, acts in ways that are contrary to the values endorsed. Rest notes this dilemma:

> Given that a person is aware of various possible courses of action in a situation, each leading to a different kind of outcome or goal, why then would a person ever choose the moral alternative, especially if it involves sacrificing some personal interest or enduring some hardship.[32]

In other words, why would one choose a particular course of action, especially if this course of action leads to personal sacrifice, an experience often encountered in situations calling for authentic response to Jesus' command "come follow me" (Mark 10:21)? More specifically, why would the adolescent assume such personal sacrifice? From a theological context we can view the adolescent's response as an authentic response of God's revealing self-communication and the deepening desire to live the Gospel. In a pastoral perspective, however, the question must also be framed psychologically. What transpires during the developmental period of adolescence that permits the adolescent to respond more fully to Jesus' question of who he is? In other words, *what developmental ex-*

perience invites the adolescent to a more authentic and personal choice to embrace discipleship?

For the adolescent, the decision to choose Christian values—to act in ways that reflect discipleship and eschew personal self-interest—can be viewed as the emergence of "moral identity." *Moral identity is the core experience of self-referencing value.* That is, moral identity is the self-revelatory understanding that "who am I" is inseparable from specific value choices. Or, to state this another way, my value choices must reflect my core value: otherwise, one lives in basic contradiction to one's own self, and becomes in the process inauthentic.

The source for one's moral identity evolves through a process whereby one's self-definition is increasingly organized, a process that is associated with the adolescent years. According to Blasi, every individual organizes a level of "self-related information" that

> determines the order and the hierarchy among the characteristics that are included in the self, along such metaphorical dimensions as central peripheral, deep superficial, important unimportant, and so on. It also defines what could be called the essential or the core self, namely, the set of those aspects without which the individual would see himself or herself to be radically different; those so central that one could not even imagine being deprived of them; those whose loss would be considered and felt as irreparable.[33]

Given this definition of moral identity, there exists not only a conscious awareness of "what I must do" and the related question, "who I must be," but the actual desire to choose actions consistent with "who I am." That is, there exists similarity between one's self-definition and personal behavior. Without this unity, a sense of self-discrepancy develops whereby, at the core level, one experiences alienation and personal estrangement. An overriding need in the psychological life of any person is the feeling of *self-consistency;* that is, values and behaviors that reflect a mutual and enduring unity.

This self-consistency between choosing what is moral and the conscious awareness of one's core definition as moral (as experienced through morally felt foundations) invites greater acceptance of personal responsibility and the motivation to strive for consistency.

A similarity exists between the notion of "moral identity" and the more commonly understood view of identity expressed in the writings of Erik Erikson. Erikson's discussion of identity is elusive. He has admitted that the term *identity* has been used indiscriminately to refer to a variety of meanings. These multiple meanings of identity include "a conscious sense of one's personal identity," "a sense of character gradually developing over time," "the synthesizing aspects of the ego," and "the growing solidarity of one's own ideas with those of the group." Although identity can take on a number of meanings, Erikson's inclination is to favor identity as a fundamental aspect of self-continuity. More specifically, then, identity formation allows one to connect a personal life history with the demands of the ongoing present while preparing for the tasks that await one in the future. More than anything, identity produces an inner sense of continuity, a cohesiveness of self. "The term identity expresses such a mutual relation in that it connotes both a persistent sameness within oneself (self-sameness) and a persistent sharing of some kind of essential character with others."[34]

According to Erikson, each developmental stage of life has a particular virtue (or what he terms "strength"). A virtue represents the successful resolution of the task essential for that particular stage. For adolescence, the stage associated with identity crisis, the positive strength corresponding to the successful meeting of identity issues is fidelity. "Fidelity is the ability to sustain loyalties freely pledged in spite of the inevitable contradictions and confusions of value systems."[35] Fidelity is, for Erikson, the "cornerstone" of identity. This definition of identity is similar to Blasi's idea of moral identity. Both definitions point out the self's capacity for an inner-directed consistency in action and the desire to direct the self toward ideals in spite of inevitable uncertainty.

Support for the notion of an adolescent moral identity is provided by probing the child and adolescent's self-understanding. For psychologist William Damon, self-understanding coincides with the notion of identity expressed above. He defines the self as a psychological construct "whose domain is the individual's experience of personal identity."[36] Specifically, Damon explores how morality relates to one's self-understanding, asking such questions as "What kind of person are you?" "What do you want out of life?" and discovering through his research a gradual schematic growth in self-understanding among children and adolescents. This self-understanding incorporates knowledge at four levels: physical (Level 1), active (Level 2), social (Level 3), and psychological (Level 4). In early childhood, self-understanding is associated with aspects of one's physical self: a young child defines himself or herself by physical characteristics and features (for example, "I am tall"). During the adolescent years, however, the social and psychological aspects of the self dominate.

> Moral self-statements are one signal of Level 4 and rarely appear in prior levels. The only real exception is some mention of reciprocal moral responsibilities sometimes made in the context of Level 3 social-relational self-statements. But morality does not become a dominant characteristic of self until Level 4, and Level 4 statements are not found in any frequency until middle adolescence.[37]

Thus, children most often characterize themselves by physical and active characteristics (the former are physical qualities whereas the latter are behaviors). Consequently, children are unable to articulate moral principles, which are typically stated by the psychological self, a self that is activated only in adolescence. To state this point another way, it is only in adolescence that a person is capable of actually expressing moral statements that authentically mirror the conscious experience of one's own core identity.

According to Damon, the adolescent self shows an increasing sensitivity toward the opinions and expectations of others. The adolescent understands that he or she must now take greater responsibility for personal behaviors and that this is an assumption that others share. This understanding grows through the presence of a "social network" in which the adolescent becomes actively engaged; he or she becomes aware of others' needs and expectations and of his or her own role within the social group.

Damon notes that a second theme of the adolescent's moral identity is the "ideological" flavor that is so often observed in adolescent thinking. With the advent of formal thinking, the adolescent discovers a framework for reflecting upon and discovering moral beliefs. From the perspective of society, adopting an ideology offers the initial underpinnings for entrance into the adult world. Although the formulation of ideology becomes more differentiated and personalized in late adolescence (the college years), the power of formal thinking allows the middle adolescent (secondary school age) to examine inchoatively, if only in a rudimentary fashion, a variety of positions on various issues. As a consequence, the adolescent develops numerous self-statements (for example, "I am a sensitive person," "I believe in being a Christian") that sow the seeds for further self-understanding in late adolescence. In other words, middle adolescence offers a fertile soil in which to plant moral positions that will be sustained, altered, or elaborated upon in the late adolescent years. Damon notes the passionate nature of adolescent thinking when he says, "perhaps at no other time in life, at least for most individuals, are such doctrines so extensively articulated and so purely held."[38]

Damon states there are two significant changes in adolescent self-understanding that provide a base for "conceptual integration with adolescent moral thinking."[39] The first shift is the development of a sophisticated Level 3 perspective on self—the social personality perspective. The adolescent now witnesses the self in a social context, which he or she soon discovers is fraught with moral consequences. Thus, "being helpful, generous, open, or suspicious all are morally relevant characteristics of one's social interactional self."[40] As the adolescent naturally interacts with peers he or she is confronted with moral questions that naturally elicit concern and which in turn assist the young person in sorting out personal moral views and right actions.

A fuller understanding of the significance of the Level 3 position of the social-interactional self is provided by psychologist James Youniss in his discussion of adolescent friendship formation. Borrowing on the work of Harry Stack Sullivan and Jean Piaget, Youniss hypothesizes that adolescents come to engage in a "relation of cooperation" out of which they grow to appreciate the thoughts and feelings of others and interact with peers in mutually supportive and healthy ways. Further, Youniss notes "the psychologically healthy and morally mature personality" is derived from this "relation of cooperation." Such relations contain five characteristics: mutuality (give and take between peers that leads to compromise and mutual understanding), standards of worth (personal judgments based on interpersonal consensus), similarity between self and others (awareness of sameness that fosters an equality in the relationship), interpersonal sensitivity (awareness of the individuality of the self and the other and the acceptance of personal limitations), and relational possibilities (the formulation of a self-definition that is derived from being in relation with others). In short, peers provide the adolescent the opportunity for increasing cooperation, developing self-insight, and greater levels of individuality. Naturally, such relationships sustained through the adolescent years nourish the growing capacity for intimacy which is increasingly felt in the late adolescent and young adult years.[41]

Psychologist Robert Kegan further confirms the social-interactional nature of the adolescent period and his observations on the development of the self add further insight to the experience of adolescence as an interactional phenomenon.[42] His constructive-developmental view of human growth situates adolescence in the "Stage 3 interpersonal self." The self at this stage is relationships. According to Kegan, the adolescent self is embedded within the interpersonal; he or she has shed the later childhood construction of the self as "need." In effect, the adolescent self no longer is its need; rather, the adolescent self has needs. As a consequence, the adolescent self can now increasingly reach out to others and regulate the self's needs through interpersonal interactions. In this new-found experience of the interpersonal, the adolescent undergoes a growing realization of the need for empathy, responsibility, and mutuality in his or her interpersonal relationships. According to Kegan, with adolescence the self becomes interactional, it becomes a shared reality. In other words, the adolescent comes to apprehend the fact that self-understanding is now situated in a reality that recognizes the needs of others.

Moving beyond this social nature of the adolescent self, another "developmental shift" occurring in the adolescent years focuses on the adolescent increasingly defining his or her self in psychological terms; this change allows the adolescent to define the self in the context of ideas and philosophical beliefs. "The system of belief [philosophical/ideological thinking] reflects the main organizing principle of the adolescent's self-conception."[43] Such beliefs have moral consequences for they frame for the adolescent a distinctive set of attitudes and behavioral norms that influence the adolescent's behavior toward others.

When the adolescent chooses a behavior he or she is in turn constructing a deepening level of self-understanding as the behavior is compared to and integrated with current levels of self-understanding. Even though Damon does not set forth a formal definition of morality, the social-interactional perspective of self implies an awareness of and focus on the welfare of others; thus, there appears to be incorporated into Damon's thinking some level of caring response toward others. Moreover, Damon's work documents the interpersonal nature of the adolescent self ("How I act towards others is who I am.") and points to the interpersonal features of the adolescent's construction of the moral self. Within this interpersonal focus there emerges a psychological understanding of self. Thus, through interactions with peers, adolescents come to view their own behaviors as either consonant or at variance with their own increasingly understood self-understandings. These self-understandings in turn are framed within philosophical and ethical understandings. Correspondingly, behaviors that vary from increasingly proclaimed self-understandings (such as "I am honest," "I am a Christian," "I am loyal to my friends") render the adolescent vulnerable to growing levels of personal dissatisfactions which must be addressed.

Having explored the nature of conscience and having defined the conscience of other-centered value, we examined the adolescent's experience of value as expressed through seven psychological dimensions. We then explored how this expression of value arises in the adolescent's everyday life experience. A diagram of the various facets of the adolescent's moral self is shown in figure 3.

An Examination of Conscience for Adolescents

This chapter has explored the development of conscience in the adolescent years. Having viewed the various developmental dynamics that constitute the human experience of conscience, we focus our attention on finding a method for applying our understanding of adolescent growth and conscience development in the service of adults who minister to youth. The method we propose is an "examination of conscience." The examination of con-

FIGURE 3

THE MORAL SELF
(The Integration of Value with the Psychological Self)

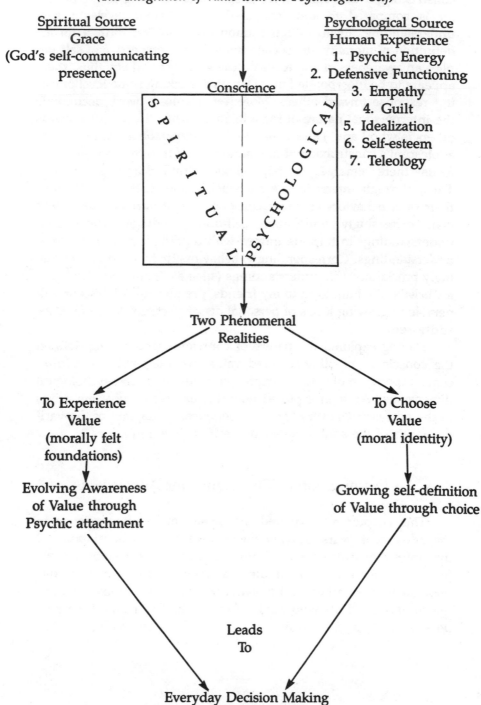

Spiritual Source
Grace
(God's self-communicating
presence)

Psychological Source
Human Experience
1. Psychic Energy
2. Defensive Functioning
3. Empathy
4. Guilt
5. Idealization
6. Self-esteem
7. Teleology

Conscience

S P I R I T U A L   P S Y C H O L O G I C A L

Two Phenomenal
Realities

To Experience
Value
(morally felt
foundations)

To Choose
Value
(moral identity)

Evolving Awareness
of Value through
Psychic attachment

Growing self-definition
of Value through choice

Leads
To

Everyday Decision Making

science has served a vital purpose in helping people reflect on their moral lives. Unfortunately, examinations are far too often rigid and moralistic and focus on rules rather than on growth and future possibility. What follows is an examination that is relevant to the adolescent's experience. Orienting moral reflection to the adolescent's developmental needs allows for more meaningful moral scrutiny and is most likely to engage the adolescent in thoughtful and searching reflection as to the quality of his or her moral life.

The examinations offered below can be used and adapted for individual counseling, retreat discussions, group gatherings, or class work. Ideally, discussion will be the starting point for deeper questions and more probing reflection on the adolescent's part. The adult minister should not hesitate to modify and expand on this list of questions and he or she should emphasize whatever areas prove most fruitful. In addition, although each examination is geared toward a specific age group (early, middle, or late adolescence) questions from the other two examinations might augment the specific focus questions used. The choice of questions depends on the age of the adolescents as well as their particular needs.

Each examination begins with a brief outline of the developmental needs of that adolescent phase and a list of questions related to the developmental needs for six focus areas. These areas are self, family, relationships, school, society, the future.

Early Adolescence

The years of junior high school (age twelve to fifteen) can be a particularly tumultuous time in the adolescent's life. These years, more than any other time in the adolescent period, are marked by confusion, self-doubt, and questioning. Pubertal changes create questions regarding one's very self. Behaviors during this period are erratic. At one moment, the adolescent might show significant regressive tendencies and resort to childhood behaviors, particularly in moments of stress and confusion. As little as one hour later, however, the adolescent at this age could manifest markedly mature actions. Adults often ask, "Is this the same child?" Cognitively, the early adolescent is often self-absorbed and appears at times oblivious of others' points of view as well as the consequences of his or her actions. Relationships during this period tend to take on more significance. Friends are viewed as sources of security and support and individual friendships begin (especially among female adolescents). Adolescents at this stage are in need of boundaries in order to help them deal with their often confused state. At this stage adolescents tend to "test the limits" in order to find out how far they might go. These challenges to adult authority are not so much attacks on adults ways and standards as they are the adolescent's attempt to establish boundaries that foster his or her own self-definition.

Self

In what ways do I see myself changing? Can I list these changes? How do I feel about the changes going on in my life right now? Are there aspects of these changes that are fearful? good? perplexing?

What are the most significant events of my childhood that I can recall? What is it like for me to leave "being a child?" Are there ways that I would like to remain a child? What "childish" parts of myself do I wish to alter? How do I relate to Saint Paul's discussion of being a child (1 Cor. 13:11). How does this verse apply to me? What is leading me to leave childhood?

What do I "feel" most deeply about? When I say I "feel" something, what do I mean? What do I find myself "thinking" about? What thoughts in particular come to my mind? What tends to preoccupy my mind? How do I waste time? Do I waste more time than I should? How might I better use some of the time that I have?

In general, how would I describe my attitude? What is my attitude toward life? the world? What is my mood usually like? What factors cause me to change my mood? Can I identify some of them? Am I susceptible to some moods more than others? Why might this be so? In what situations am I most likely to be happy? sad? fearful? serious?

What do I have to be "thankful" about? How do I show this thankfulness? How am I grateful to others?

Do I pray? What are the feelings I have when I talk to God? What is my image of God? Father? Mother? Protector? Adult? Friend? Judge? Is Jesus a friend to me? In what ways is Jesus a friend? What responsibility do I take on in this relationship if I describe Jesus as a friend? Does he console me? protect me? comfort me? challenge me? What questions do I have about Jesus? What do I do for Jesus in return?

Do I find myself being self-conscious? In what areas of my life am I self-conscious? Do I sometimes feel that others are watching me? Do I spend too much time being preoccupied with myself? If I could change some things about myself what would I change? What do these changes say about my values?

Do I make excuses for my behavior? Would people who know me call me a responsible person? Would they call me a loving person? Can I be honest with myself about what I do and what I think? In what areas of my life do I need to grow so that I can be the kind of person I want to be? Am I critical of others? Am I overly critical of others?

Do questions of drug and alcohol abuse arise in my life? How do I handle these questions? Do I use alcohol and other drugs? Why do I use them? What do they do for me? Am I aware of the effects and consequences of using these drugs?

What are my thoughts and feelings about sexuality? What are the values I think of when questions of sexuality and sexual behavior surface? Do I have values in this area of my life? What are my underlying feelings when I talk about sexual matters?

Family

What is it like for me to be a son or daughter? What is it like to be an adolescent in my family? How does being an adolescent in this family change my relationship with other family members? How is my relationship with other family members changing: mom? dad? brothers? sisters? What are the experiences of my family that I am grateful for? What experiences do I find most difficult? painful? How do I contribute to making my family a good and happy place? If there is hurt and pain in my family, do I have someone with whom I can share these feelings?

How do I value the members of my family? Are there particular members of my family with whom I do not get along? Who am I most like in my family? Most different from? Can I forgive members of my family? To what extent is there jealousy of others in my family? How do I appreciate members of my family? How do I care for members of my family?

Can I allow others in my family to grow and change just as I am growing and changing? Do I stereotype others in my family? How is my relationship with family members different from when I was six? ten? What accounts for this change?

Relationships

How do I define the word *friend*? What does it mean for someone to be my friend? Who are my friends? What are the values that I appreciate in my friends? How do I show my friends that I appreciate them? How do I let my friends care for me? How do I care for them?

What does having a particular person as a friend do for me? What is the most significant thing that a friend can do for another friend? How is Jesus part of my friendships with others? Would Jesus approve of my friends? Why? Why not?

Do I belong to a group? What values do we share in the group? Would Jesus be welcome in my group? What role do I take on in my group? Why is this group important for me? Can members in this group disagree? Can I be my own person in the group? Are there ways that I can be different from the group?

School

Is my school a better place because of me? How do I show respect and care for classmates? teachers? staff? Am I grateful for the opportunity to learn? Do I use my talents to the best of my abilities? Am I honest in school? Am I loyal to my school? my class? Do I sometimes stereotype other classes and schools?

Society

Do I have interests outside my home? What interests me about my country? my state? my city? the world? Do I ever think of myself as becoming an active and responsible citizen? What does this mean for me? What type of values should a citizen in America have?

Future

What are my "dreams" for the future? Am I a hopeful person? In what do I hope? What are my feelings when I think about the future? How can I start preparing for my future even now?

Middle Adolescence

The predominant question of the middle adolescent years is, Who am I? Questions of identity preoccupy the secondary school student age fifteen to eighteen. For the most part, behavior during these years is more consistent than that of the early adolescent years. Middle adolescents usually form more stable and focused relationships with both sexes. Ethical and value questions start to arise for many adolescents, and their newly acquired cognitive skills are put to the test by means of deeper questioning and reflection. The social life of the middle adolescent is expanded and there is often a passage to more adult responsibilities with such activities as dating, first job, or driving. Career goals are sometimes more in focus as the adolescent begins to look toward the future.

Self

How would I define myself? If my friends had to write a definition of me, what would they say? What values are important to my self-definition? Do my behaviors reflect these values?

What are the roles that I experience in my life (son or daughter, worker, student, athlete, friend)? Do these roles sometimes conflict with one another? If so, how do I handle these conflicts?

What place does prayer occupy in my life? How has my relationship with Jesus changed over the past few years? How close would I say I am to Jesus? What do I share with him? Do I hold back? Can I be honest with him about my feelings? Do I feel I belong to the church? Do I have a faith community or support group in which I can talk about my faith? Are there serious questions that I have regarding faith and values? Would I consider myself a person who has faith? What does faith mean to me? How do I find support for my faith? How do I support others in their faith?

Whom do I admire in my life? Whom do I look up to? Whom do I respect? Why do I respect these people? Do I feel myself more of an adult? Do I want to take on adult responsibility? Are there parts of being an adult that I fear? What are these areas?

How am I becoming more responsible in my life? Am I developing a personal philosophy for my life?

What place do drugs and alcohol occupy in my life? Are using drugs important for me? Why do I use drugs? Are there things I might be avoiding by my drug use? How does using drugs or alcohol reflect my values? contradict my values?

What are my feelings about being a man or a woman? How comfortable am I with members of the opposite sex? Do I have questions about my sexuality? Do I have someone I can discuss with this area of my life? Do I stereotype members of the opposite sex? Do I sometimes feel I "have" to behave in a certain way because I am a man? a woman?

Family

How is my role in the family changing? How am I treated in the family? What are the sources of love and happiness in my family? The sources of conflict and hurt? What roles do I play in each of these situations? How am I grateful to others in my family for their lives? Do I sometimes find myself doing things just to be different from others in my family? Do I treat others in my family with the same respect that I wish they would give to me?

Relationships

Do I have a best friend? What makes this person a best friend? What are the values I most admire in a friend? How honest am I in my friendships? Do I try to control my friends? Do I respect the confidences and privacy of others? Am I sometimes jealous of others? Can I forgive others when they hurt me? How do I care for others? Does being a Christian say anything to me about being a friend? In other words, if I wasn't a Christian would I behave or feel differently toward my friends?

When I think of sexual expression of my feelings, what are the values that I associate with it? What role does honesty? fidelity? commitment? trust? have in sexual expression? Is self-control something I see as important? How does being a Christian influence or affect my sexual behavior? How do manipulation, dishonesty, and exploitation become part of sexual expression? Why do I think this is so?

School

How do I utilize my talents in school? How is school a better place because of me? How do I show respect for other students?

teachers? staff? Do I have goals? self-discipline? How might I use my learning to help others? How has my schooling influenced the values that I hold? Do I stereotype others in my class? other classes? other schools? Do I sometimes get so involved in some projects or events that I don't have time for other activities and interests?

Society

What type of interest do I have in affairs involving my city? state? nation? world? Am I becoming more aware of social problems? What thoughts and opinions am I forming about politics? candidates? social issues? What type of values are reflected in these interests? How would I define being a good citizen?

Do I have a part-time job? Do I treat my employer justly? What have I learned about myself and my values from my work experience?

Future

Have I thought about college? work? career? How am I preparing myself for my future? What values are reflected in my career choice? What are my goals in life?

Late Adolescence

The undergraduate college years are a time for further consolidation of identity needs. Questions of commitment are more directly faced by the late adolescent. Increasingly, intimacy needs come to the forefront and relationships take on special significance. The late adolescent slowly begins to develop a more coherent (yet often still forming) philosophy of life. Ethical questions and widening interests preoccupy the adolescent's time.

Self

As I look back over the past few years of my life, what do I find easiest to accept about myself? Are there aspects of myself that I have yet to accept?

As I reflect back to my early years as an adolescent what would I describe as the most significant experiences of my life? Why?

What do I say that I need still to explore? to understand? to feel? In what areas of my life do I still need to grow?

How has my life become more loving? How do I nourish and sustain my capacity for love?

What decisions have I made for my life? What criteria do I use to make these decisions? What values are part of these decisions?

How do I take care of myself? Do I find time for solitude? for prayer? How do I support my faith life? Do I have the desire to know myself more and more? How am I "true to myself"?

Family

What is the "quality" of my relationship with my family? What experiences of my family do I most cherish? What values of my family have I adopted for my own? What values have I sought to ignore or alter? Why? How has each member of my family influenced me? Can I forgive members of my family? Can I ask for forgiveness?

Relationships

Who are the people that I most value in life? Why? What have each of the significant relationships in my life given me? What have I given them?

How do I express commitment in relationships? What are the values that I associate with commitment? In what ways do specific relationships in my life still need to grow? How do I handle conflict in my relationships? How does being a Christian influence my relationships? Can I experience the relationships in my life as gifts from God? How am I thankful for these gifts?

School

What has college allowed me to reflect upon in my life? How is the quality of my reflection and depth of my thinking changed because of my college experience? Whom have I come to value most because of my college experience? Why do I value these people?

Society

How have my college years or work experience broadened my interests? Do I have a philosophy of life? What are the defining features of this worldview that I have? What role do I hope to play in terms of civic responsibility and commitment? What values do I give priority to when I take positions on issues? What is my "hope" for my country? How do I see myself as a "just" man or woman?

Future

If I were to look back twenty years from now, what would I hope to have accomplished? What are my goals for the future? What will others say about me? What would I want others to say about me? How am I preparing myself even now so that what I desire might come true?

Conclusion

This chapter has looked at the psychological dimensions of conscience with an eye toward more fully understanding the significance of conscience in the lives of adolescents. Moreover, the explanation of conscience offered in these pages differs substantially from other approaches to moral development offered by theorists such as Kohlberg. Below are listed what I view to be the advantages of the approach I have described.

First, this approach is radically *developmental*. By developmental I mean that it appreciates the life experience of the adolescent *as* an adolescent. It is sensitive to the actual ongoing functioning and dynamics that are part of the adolescent's life experience. And, as I consistently have argued in these pages, God's self-communicating presence is offered only in the ongoing reality of one's developmental stage of life. As such, a developmental focus recognizes the adolescent's crucial need to respond to significant life goals in a maturing fashion and to commit the necessary psychic resources to such ends. Likewise, our view of conscience calls for sufficient self-mastery to allow the young person to search continually for what is maturing and true. Within this process of growth there exists a continual appropriation of freedom and responsibility for life decisions that reflect the response to God's self-communication. In sum, any model of conscience must be radically rooted in the ongoing developmental experiences of the person inasmuch as any search for value and corresponding decision for value can only arise from one's current developmental level.

Equally important is the fact that this model of conscience is essentially *hopeful*. The model we propose never rests on how conscience is currently functioning. Rather, it offers a foundation for seeking future responses that are more fundamentally loving and caring while at the same time growthful and developmentally sound. In this regard, conscience is an evolving dynamic of growing love. The idealizing quality we propose as a dimension of conscience continually appropriates more adequate images, ideals, and understandings that increase awareness of and need for care and concern.

Because our view of conscience appreciates the developmental level of personhood, it contributes to a *realistic* account of one's attributes. The impetus for this realism is contained within the forming of maturing defenses that maintain adequate psychic functioning (and thus a realistic response to reality): one becomes increasingly capable of facing the darkness, and the unexplored and limited nature of one's own self. Moreover, the vital experience of guilt serves as a reminder of the frailty of the moral self. As we have described it, moral guilt functions as an enduring mechanism for self-honesty. It springs forth as a reminder of the need for a humble stance. As a consequence, it offers a sense of deepening gratitude to the Lord, who blesses us, offers his grace, and comforts us still.

The final advantage of this view of conscience is the foundation it provides for *praxis*. Empathy continually nurtures our sensitivities to the sufferings of others and serves as a catalyst for the motivation to aid and care for others. Moral guilt, too, provides a vital role in this response to others' needs. A teleological perspective offers the continual self-awareness for purposive meaning, greater clarification, and the assuming of personal responsibility for action. Idealizations channel our psychic investments in other-centered values, which forges increasing self-consistency between "who I am" and "what I do." Further, this idealizing quality serves as a harbinger for images and visions of future endeavors that more and more appropriate the ideal (see Matt. 16: 24–26). In all of this dynamic undertaking, there exists the capacity for suffering. Indeed, an essential quality of the Christian notion of conscience is the appropriation of value that accepts the reality of suffering. Christian praxis includes the reality of suffering. Indeed, the vision of the Christian message understands the nature of self-sacrifice and what it entails—to offer oneself for continual efforts to care and share with others. The dimensions we have offered as central to conscience make this capacity for suffering humanly intelligible. For one, the idealizations drawn forth through psychic investment hearten loyalty and fidelity and the capacity to endure suffering. The values expressed in and the ideals which spring from idealization continually thrust into consciousness the questions, "Who am I to be?" and "What am I to become?" They continually beckon forth images and visions, nurtured within the community of faith, that sustain the desire, in the midst of self-doubt and suffering, to gradually become more wholly that vision. In sum, the model of conscience we propose helps us to appreciate the need for developmental sensitivity, the capacity for hopefulness and a future orientation, the necessity for humility and gratefulness, and the essential nature of praxis and sustained and enduring service, even at the price of ongoing self-sacrifice.

This elaboration of conscience provides, furthermore, a response to the definition of adolescent morality that we offered in chapter 1. Recall that we sought a definition that was sensitive to the developmental level of the adolescent, appreciated the various struggles and dimensions of the adolescent's experience, was realistically yet future oriented, and was sensitive to the environment and the need for ongoing nurturance and care. The dimensions of conscience that we set forth seek to address these crucial points.

This view of conscience, likewise, provides a foundation for the model of morality offered by Rest (see chapter 2). Some moral thinkers view conscience in what might be termed structural categories. That is, they look upon conscience as composed of various levels. An advantage to this approach is that it provides some conceptual clarity. The limitation of this approach, however, is that it can inhibit the sense of dynamism that is so essential for understanding conscience. Thus, I hesitate to consider conscience in terms of such categories. Rather, I prefer to view it as an ongoing dynamic of love, with the various dimensions operating together in a synergistic fashion to lead one to greater appropriation of the Gospel's command to love. Thus, a metaphor that most aptly applies is that of "fuel" or "energy." In this respect, conscience fuels one's decisions and the accompanying reflection and human action to take on a more and more loving stance. Rest's model helps us to see how this takes place.

Recall that Rest offered a model of morality that contained four components: sensitivity (which points to awareness and understanding of a situation); judgment (arriving at what is moral); planning (choosing and formulating value based on realism); and executing (proceeding to act on one's choice). The dimensions of conscience we have offered energize these four components. That is, conscience has been defined as the realization and choosing of other-centered value in one's concrete life situation. I view the Rest model as an excellent way, from a psychological perspective, to delineate how this might be done.

How might we relate the psychological dynamics of conscience formation to Rest's model? Given our definition of conscience as the realization and choosing of value, it can easily fit into Rest's second and third components. However, the way we have proposed conscience allows for the embracing of all four components. The dimensions of conscience that we have set forth emphasize sensitivity to moral needs, awareness of what is moral, the choosing of value, and the actual carrying out of one's moral intentions (praxis). Thus, I would view the dimensional nature of conscience as described in these pages as providing the energy for the Rest model. To state this another way, if Rest's model serves as a way to explore morality, then conscience as we defined it energizes each of Rest's four components. Conscience is the dynamic process that fuels each of the components to be actualized at an optimal level. In short, conscience sensitizes us to moral issues at hand. It further leads us to choose specific values while calling forth from us a praxis orientation.

Throughout these pages we have sought to frame value as not only something we believe, but as a reality that we choose and carry out; in essence, the area of decision making. It is to this dynamic of choice that we now turn.

CHAPTER FOUR

Helping Adolescents
Make Moral Decisions

In the preceding chapter we explored the framework of the adolescent moral self. In this chapter we turn to the actual making of moral decisions and explore both the dynamic of adolescent moral decision making and possible strategies that religious professionals can employ to further the development of the adolescent's moral self.

I would like to offer a metaphor for the various facets of our approach. When one looks at a flower one can be struck by its beauty. No doubt many things contribute to this perception. The flower appears well-proportioned and perfectly shaped; individual parts of the flower, such as the petals and stem, serve to reinforce the flower's beauty; the striking colors and fragrance add to the flower's attractiveness. Even so, the flower's appeal depends upon other realities. There exists, for example, the need for nutrients, fertile soil, and adequate climate. In short, our fascination with the flower depends upon many features. Something else, however, arises from our perception. Above and beyond the essential ingredients needed to allow the flower to flourish and the discrete elements that together give the flower its striking appearance, there exists a certain "quality" to the flower. We are left with a feeling of wonder and awe.

This same phenomenon arises when we reflect on the moral life. Like the flower, there exist fundamental parts to the moral life. When we say someone is moral, we refer to a general quality; yet there are also discrete elements. Such a person most likely possesses a definite reflective capacity and a great deal of sensitivity (empathy) to the feelings and needs of others. Environment can nourish a deepening moral sense: just as the flower needs adequate weather and soil, so, too, does a person need the presence of others as role models and a supportive environment that encourages sensitivity and right acts. Finally, like the flower, we have the experience of some intangible features. When we refer to someone as moral we refer to a certain quality of the person. When we relate to such a person we are struck by a quality that is most aptly labeled integrity. Integrity is not something we can simply point to; it is something that exists because of who this person is in his or her life. However, there is something that confirms our identification of this person as a person of integrity. When we describe someone as a person of integrity, what we rely on are the decisions that this man or woman makes. When we say someone has moral integrity what we refer to is an essential trust that the decisions of this person's life flow from and reflect the moral self and the workings of conscience. It is a belief that this person's conscious identity is inseparably linked to a core awareness of value, and that he or she makes these values present through decisions.

The Adolescent Experience

Decisions are especially problematic for adolescents because their world is in flux and their understanding of the world is marked by an increasing need to sort out the complexities of their everyday lives. For the adolescent,

> transitions represent an increase in the number and complexity of relationship-oriented tasks—for example, dealing with friends in a group context, changing classes in a high school environment, establishing working relationships with employers, and maintaining family ties despite increasing autonomy from parents.[1]

In essence, their world is a transitional world wherein old patterns of relating and thinking are gradually shed or altered. At the same time, the mystery of "adulthood" and its meaning proves elusive and is far off, often not truly completed in an adequately functioning way until the midtwenties.

In chapter 2 we noted that research indicates that the subjective experience of adolescents is sometimes one of drifting:

The problem is that adolescents often have no meaningful goals. They have not had the time to attach themselves to anything they consider worthwhile. As a result, nothing is challenging to them, and their skills fall into disuse. Entropy takes the form of a meaningless waste of time. Being overwhelmed and being unchallenged have common elements. They both represent states of imbalance between a person and the world. In one case the world offers too much, in the other too little. Underlying them both is a breakdown in a person's ability to control his or her actions—to set meaningful goals, define limits and provide and receive feedback.[2]

This insightful comment by researchers Csikszentmihalyi and Larson addresses an essential predicament of adolescence. As we have indicated in an earlier chapter, these writers note that adolescents face a continual struggle with "psychic entrophy" which is characterized by bad moods, passivity, lack of motivation, and unfocused attention.[3] None of these qualities are in and of themselves debilitating (for example, a bad mood could lead one to spend time in valuable reflection and self-examination and the facing of one's personal struggles). However, over time, the continual display of troubled feelings channels the adolescent's energies away from purposeful and engaging activities. Adolescents who are unable to order their experience, learn from their mistakes, and engage their world in constructive fashion, deprive themselves of the vital learning experiences required for a productive and meaningful adulthood. Adolescents who are unable to attend to necessary life tasks and reflect on the consequences of their behaviors are at a disadvantage when faced with both everyday and major life decisions. Lacking goals and a firm sense of purpose, these adolescents dissipate their energies; the result is a fragile sense of purpose or a poor understanding of their lives and where they are going.

I have found in my own clinical-pastoral work with adolescents that one of the experiences most disruptive to sound and growthful decision making is the adolescent's subjective experience of loneliness. "Loneliness resembles hunger both as an experience and as a motivational force: It calls attention to a painful deficit, and it spurs one to put an end to it."[4]

The feeling of loneliness is subjectively distressful, particularly in adolescence. This increased distress is most likely due to the intrapsychic conflicts and the newly experienced intensity of the adolescent's emotional experience.

> Adolescents may not be more lonely than people at other points of transition in their lives, but there are common elements to the adolescent process that give loneliness at this stage a specific quality. Characteristically, loneliness during adolescence is stamped with issues of mourning one's own identity as a child and giving up certain forms of childhood attachments and beliefs. The process of separating and maturing is tinged with loneliness.[5]

Loneliness directly influences the capacity of the adolescent to make maturing decisions. Experiencing an impoverished inner self resulting from the lack of validation from others (a direct result of loneliness), an adolescent might be prone to yield his or her own judgment to that of the group in order to gain acceptance. In other instances, the relationship between two adolescents is compromised when decisions about the integrity of the relationship and the very care of the other is damaged by rationalized motives or needy responses whose true aim is to "fill up" feelings of emotional deficiency (an often common experience in sexual expression among adolescents). Equally important, sensitivity to others can often be compromised by the adolescent's too frequent focus on his or her own needs. Still other adolescents take the approach of making impulsive and foolish choices in order to soothe inner feelings of impoverishment.

The inward focus that loneliness fosters and its accompanying negative moods suggest that many adolescents become preoccupied with their own emotional state and are unable to sustain and provide the needed awareness required for relating to others.

The fundamental task for all humans, regardless of age, is to grow. "To grow means to learn to interact with more and more complex dimensions of reality."[6] Unfortunately, the experiences of many adolescents lead them to disregard such learning. As we have noted, many adolescents are preoccupied with moods that lead them to draw inward or withdraw from the world they cannot engage. Other adolescents have yet to establish a reasonable level of control over their urges and wage an ongoing battle with their own impulses. Another way that learning is diminished is through the complexity of society, which intimidates and at times overwhelms the adolescent. Lacking skills, adequate time for reflection, and with no way to process or set up goals and sound choices, many adolescents flee the tasks necessary to foster their own growth.

Many adolescents experience a lack of goals and meaning in their lives. Instead, their energies are all too often dissipated by fleeting tasks that sap the psychic energy needed for maturation. Adolescents often do not know how to focus, attend, choose, or prioritize goals. Their time is all too often spent in distracting activities (for example, excessive television watching) or in some cases injurious ones (like drug abuse). Their lack of concentration, motivation, and focus dilutes the essential questions that weigh on them: "Who are you?" "What are you becoming?" (It should be pointed out here that some adolescents can become too goal centered and focused. This is sometimes found among adolescents from middle-class and achievement-oriented families. Although the manifestations are different, in these cases one also finds distraction from other important facets of their selves.)

Framing Choices for the Adolescent Experience

The adolescent's tendency to dissipate psychic energies weakens the moral self. We have conceptualized the moral self as the multidimensional integration and flow of conscience in the adolescent's everyday life. This moral self incorporates increasing realization of and decision for values that are decidedly other-centered. Recall that the first dimension of conscience dealt with utilizing psychic energy in growthful and maturing ways (this was explored as a healthy attachment and attention to developmental tasks). The adolescent who is at the mercy of his or her impulses or who fritters away, misuses, or exhausts psychic energy is apt not to develop the capacity to reflect on and discern the need for other-centered values nor to have the resolute will that is required for making or carrying out choices.

Given this situation, what is the role of the adult ministering to youth? I believe that the role of the adult is that of helping the adolescent to "frame" choices. I purposely use the word "frame." The word "frame" invites the use of an image as well as offering a structure. These two emphases—image and structure—hold the key to helping adolescents make moral decisions. An image implies some type of picture. Moreover, an image elicits an imaginative dimension that evokes feelings as the image takes on specific meanings. To utilize structure, on the other hand, is to provide order, clarity, and purpose.

When assessing the subjective state of adolescence, researchers Csikszentmihalyi and Larson note:

> In our research we could not observe how teenagers go through the steps of building a permanent set of goals that would serve to give purpose and meaning to their lives. This is a slow process, with many stops and starts. Only a few adolescents actually develop fully authentic life goals—most are satisfied to pursue the goals society prescribes: a college education, a job, marriage, children, and life within conventional standards of morality.[7]

These researchers remark that a critical component for finding meaning and purpose in life arises from the development of a "life theme." A life theme is a set of goals which provide one's life with meaning and purpose. It serves as an overarching umbrella that renders intelligibility to one's everyday experience and gives order to the multitude of experiences which we encounter. A life theme allows one to endure hardship and self-sacrifice; this is possible because it provides meaning and renders inviolable one's deepest desires. As noted, adolescents are remarkably remiss at developing life themes. This is not all that surprising given their developmental level, the demands made upon them, and the complexity of the realities they encounter. Still, adolescence is an opportune time for beginning to sort out the meanings and significance of life. Adolescence is a fertile soil into which the ideals and enduring purposes of life take root. Mature adulthood requires a rooted and enduring life purpose which presents guiding principles for one's decisions and behaviors.

I would like to take the notion of life theme and view it in a broader perspective as a fundamental response to life's realities. In other words, we respond to life through an orientation, or life theme, that defines and interprets our experiences.

The fundamental orientation (life theme) of the Christian is contained in the inescapable fact of God's love for me. "Love, then, consists in this: not that we have loved God but that he has loved us" (1 John 4:10). The piercing truth of this passage is God's love for me "as I am." We do not merit this love through achievements and mastery, it is simply there, always offered with no questions asked. The spiritual writer Tony DeMello captures this truth when he asks, "What does he see in me that even though he knows my sinfulness, he says 'You are precious to my heart'?"[8]

God's love for me, in sum, is the pervasive and foundational life theme that orients, sustains, and nourishes my life. Yet, this life theme has a corollary: the complement of God's love is our response. What flows from the experience of this guiding theme of being loved is our grateful response of service. As Ignatius notes, "God creates me out of love which desires nothing more than a return of love on my part. So much does he love me that even though I take myself away from him, he continues to be my Savior and Redeemer."[9] In the response we make to God's love there is the need to "order" our affections. Affections are more than emotions. Affections serve as the complete response of self as a loving person to God's offering of grace. In other words, affections are my emotions, my will, my desires, my physical self—my total self responding to God's offer of grace. Ignatius speaks of affections as ordered when our love for people, places, or things and their use is deeply rooted in God. All that exists is loved and ordered through God's love and we in turn must love all creation in and through God. Thus, ordered affection disposes me to love all things properly—in and through God.

A critical question at this point becomes: How is the fundamental life theme of being loved and responding in gratitude made relevant for the life of the adolescent? It is here that the adult's "intrusive" presence becomes important as a source of framing for the adolescent. If we as adults are to engage adolescents in the task of sound moral decision making, then it is important that our framing enable the adolescent to look beyond a mere discussion of words and endless debate on rules and regulations (although guidelines are imperative for the adolescent). Our task is to engage the adolescent in forming life themes, with the fundamental life theme being the love of God and the call to service. Other life themes as they develop (career choices, a philosophy of life, avocations) must reflect this fundamental life theme. Furthermore, the adolescent's response to this life theme must move beyond an intellectual discussion. (A real shortcoming I find with Kohlberg's method is that it keeps the discussion of morality on an intellectual level.)

The adolescent needs engagement at the imaginative level. Contemporary theology has come to view imagination as a vital source for seeking truth and discerning the presence of God's self-communication. Imagination serves as an entrance for deeper perceptions, sensitivity, and openness. Imagination encourages a perceptive sensitivity to the reality at hand and the underlying meanings of events that are significant for my life.

Imaginative experience focuses on selected aspects of experience. It singles out certain features of an experience or situation and focuses on them, gleaning in the process the deepening reality of the experience. Imagination, moreover, provides for new insights; from our images flow forth new ways of perceiving and understanding. Imagination also supports our creative endeavors as we link different realities into a new way of viewing.

Finally, imagination exists as an integrative product of cognitive, emotional, and motivational features of our experience. Its cognitive dimension arises from the insight and understanding that it provides. The images we savor, likewise, elicit our emotional involvement. And lastly, an image can stir us to a new way of behaving as we attempt to preserve its integrity. In short, we seek to emulate the values and meaning that the image displays.

Moralist Philip Keane has provided a penetrating insight into the use of moral imagination in Christian life. In defining the imagination, he notes that

> imagination can be described as the basic process by which we draw together the concrete and the universal elements of our human experience. With imagination we let go of any inadequate preconceived notions of how the abstract and the concrete relate to one another. We suspend judgment about how to unite the concrete and the abstract. We let the two sides of our knowing play with one another. By allowing this interplay between the two aspects of our knowing, we get a much deeper chance to look at what we know, to form a vision of it.[10]

In Keane's view, the various experience of our lives "play" with one another. The purpose of this play "is to lead us to better, more sound judgments."[11] Play serves as a way to seek the deeper truth and unity in our experience; in short, imagination solidifies deeper meanings within us. Imagination can be regarded as the solidifying force that enables the life theme of God's love to permeate all of our experiences—whether they be relationships, intellectual undertakings, creative endeavors, or self-discovery through new experiences. Imagination works as a unifying force, blending the realities of our lives in a coherent fashion in order that God's love is understood and is present at this moment in our life.

The imagining of God's love takes on a special significance in the rooted reality of one's life history. For each person, the foundational life theme of God's love takes root in the capacity for reflecting on one's own life as a gift from God. The spiritual writer John English refers to this reality when he writes of the consolation of one's life history. He notes,

> "Consolation" is more than a good feeling or pleasant experience. Consolation has that special spiritual meaning of being drawn towards God in a love that knows and loves all beings in the ambit of this love. "Did not our hearts burn within us as he opened up the scriptures to us?" (Luke 24:32).[12]

This consolation allows for my life to be experienced as a uniquely personal experience of God's love:

> it personalizes my decisions, my actions, my social and Christian life. Moreover, this consolation carries with it the element of uniqueness; the continual need to make decisions requires a guide such as the consolation arising out of this consciousness.[13]

The consciousness of a life theme rooted in the awareness and felt experience of God's radical love is the foundational soil for any approach to adolescent moral decision making. Adults ministering to adolescents should have as one of their main goals aiding the adolescent in developing the conscious realization of this consolation. By adolescence, young people are able to view their lives in thematic and story form. They can perceive significant characters and themes and comprehend a temporal perspective to their own growth. Still, the task of helping adolescents to experience the Lord's consolation remains difficult. Cultural influences and the ravaging of family life that has become so much a part of the cultural landscape have clearly made difficult the "feeling" of being loved and accepted. When I give workshops on adolescence I am continually struck by questions from educators and youth workers that speak of the problems of youth who lack self-esteem and who experience difficult and in some cases traumatic home and family problems.

I had a clear example of this in my own clinical work. I was assigned as the therapist to a high school adolescent named Ann (the name of course is altered to protect confidentiality). Ann's life had been brutal. She had been physically and sexually abused. Her mother had died tragically. She had experimented and abused a wide variety of drugs. There was little if anything in her life that she felt grateful for. I was seeing her as a psychologist rather than as a priest, hence, explicit references to God's love and her experience of God received little mention, though we did discuss her own moral views on various matters and feelings toward religion. I pondered how to make real the fact that there were, indeed, in her life moments of gratefulness and consolation. I learned that it was my acceptance of Ann as Ann and my ability to tolerate her acting out, her angry spells, and her hostility that enabled me to work with her. More than anything, Ann needed an adult who could accept her for who she was, in the midst of her own pain and hurt.

At the same time, I realized that Ann was still an adolescent, in every sense of the term. She still had the same tendencies and needs that preoccupy every adolescent. She still needed the intrusive presence of adults to challenge her simplistic and at times distorted thinking. Even though her life had been hard, indeed tragic, there were still moments of gratefulness (a letter, a smile from someone on the ward, the opportunity to do something). Equally important, she still needed challenge. There is a great temptation in ministry to adolescents at both the high school and college levels to be with them in their hurt and to avoid the need for challenge. Both are important and each has its place. Over the years I have become more and more convinced that the developmental tendencies of adolescence require the presence of adults who *actively engage* adolescents, help them see a wider perspective, encourage them to explore other ways of perceiving, and question shortsighted and at times clearly wrong attitudes and behaviors. This of course must be done in sensitive ways; yet, it must be done. Adult members of faith communities have an obligation to intrude into the life space and consciousness of youth. The reality always is before us: If we as adults do not become significant catalysts for adolescent and young adult growth, then by default cultural and other influences will be the significant and defining presence in young peoples' lives. Ministry and care for adolescents does not mean not challenging them. Rather, it means accepting them for who they are, as loved by God, and to be expressions of that love through care and a continual source for helping them to see how they must continue to grow and develop in their lives through the taking of responsibility.

We have stated that the adult's presence in the adolescent's life is that of one who "frames" questions for the adolescent through image and structure. In turn, this framing should underscore the significance of the adolescent's felt experience of consolation. I think that image making is immensely helpful in aiding adolescents to understand their own lives and to provide insight for their moral growth. There are many varieties of image making:

1. Some images I have used in my own work with adolescents include having them dream of who they are becoming and to reflect on the values present in this process.

2. Another image is to have adolescents imagine a perfect world and what it would be like, and to explore with them their own role in forming and helping to build such a world.

3. Since adolescents are often preoccupied with the immediate events in their life I have found it profitable to have an adolescent focus just on a "day." To reflect on all that has happened and to sort out the unexpected and the grateful moments. Quite often these are experiences that have received little attention: a smile from a friend or an opportunity to join a club or sports team. Everyday experiences—of parents, school, or health—are too often taken for granted.

4. One image I have found useful is to have an adolescent imagine that his or her friends are by a well. The friends draw up the bucket, which represents a gift or attribute the adolescent wishes to be for his or her friends. What do the friends encounter when they draw up the bucket?

5. Another helpful image is to have the adolescent image himself or herself as a gift or present to someone. Describe the gift.

What does the gift say about the adolescent? What does the adolescent wish to convey to others by being this gift?

The above are just some of the examples which can be used with adolescents. Images and imagination provide the adolescent with "another way of seeing"; in effect, images provide insight and new understandings of the moral self.

Just as the adult helps frame images for the adolescent, he or she can also frame a structure. This is accomplished through questions that orient the adolescent to reflect on his or her behaviors. Some questions I have found helpful in this regard include, What are you becoming by this [name the behavior]? Who will you be in five years or ten years if this continues?

Still other questions include, What is your dream for life? How are you living this dream now?

—What do you think God is asking of you now?

—How is this making you who you are? Is this what you want to be?

—What is your hope for the future?

—Where do you think God is leading you? What signs does he give you that this is the path to follow?

An Overall Framework for Adolescent Moral Decision Making

We have come to the point in the discussion where we need to focus on an overall framework for adolescent decision making. In order to examine this process of decision making we will utilize Rest's model of morality as outlined in chapter 2. We will offer questions that refer to the fundamental life theme of God's love and the adolescent's experience of gratefulness and service. At the same time, we will keep in mind the dimensions of conscience, outlined in chapter 3, which served as an energizing source and fuel for each of Rest's four dimensions.

An outline of the adolescent decision making process is shown in figure 4. As we see in the outline, decision making is a dynamic process in the growth of the adolescent's moral self. That is, once made, decisions become grist for the development of further decisions. As decisions are made, they become catalysts for developing the adolescent's awareness of moral identity. Decisions either validate the conscious selfimage ("I am moral"—because I have made this choice) or they lead to renegotiation of the adolescent's meaning of moral as new decisions are integrated with previous choices and interpretive meanings of being moral.

Figure 4 seeks to include the other factors that sustain or inhibit the development of the moral self. These include developmental and personal strengths and weaknesses, environmental and communal support, and the presence of the "intrusive" adult who helps to frame the adolescent's moral search. There are adolescents who experience significant psychological impairment, such as impulsivity or crippling deficits in self-esteem, thereby being unable to attend adequately in a reflective way to moral issues. Other adolescents might be so "needy" that they are simply unable to resist temptation and morally questionable behaviors. Likewise, the adolescent who is brought up in a home where his or her views are never given consideration or where there is harsh and punitive reactions to misbehavior is almost invariably limited in his or her capacity to attend adequately to moral decision making. The reader might be struck by the addition of "extraneous factors" such as poverty, lack of opportunities, or even luck. This in no way implies that an adolescent from an impoverished background cannot grow to develop a remarkably "moral" life. In fact, I have personally encountered this in some adolescents. Nor does it imply that those who are relatively well off will be moral. The psychological problems and yuppy attitudes of many middle- and upper-middle class homes prove the limits of material resources. What I do suggest, however, is that the adolescent who is limited in his or her experiences (lack of travel opportunities, worry about finances at home, and the like) might have a harder time being *able* to attend to some issues simply because he or she might need to "survive." In such an environment, defenses must be strong and growth-producing experiences might be limited.

Some readers might also take issue with the presence of the variable "luck." I am more and more convinced that luck is involved in the development of everyone's life. The reader need only think about a certain teacher or some other figure he or she remembers. How did one come to know this person? Chances are that one just happened to be in this class rather than that one, this dormitory floor rather than another, here rather than there. Luck, indeed, does play a role in the evolution of all aspects of the self. Some things simply happen when they will happen.

Adolescents encounter numerous instances where they are asked to make moral choices. A brief listing of these might include the following: breaking confidences of a friend, sexual involvement, cheating, self-damaging behaviors (for example, drug abuse), putting others at risk through one's own risky behaviors, stereotyping others, uncharitable attitudes at home, and breaking established rules. If anything, this list points out that adolescents, like everyone else, are continually challenged to respond to their conscience and to reflect by their attitudes and behavior the call to other-centered value.

It is simply not possible to describe a "typical" situation in which one can accurately delineate the multiple facets that go into any one adolescent's decision at any one time. However, we have offered through Rest's model a perspective of four critical components that give us insight into the adolescent's moral decision. In any decision that the adolescent might have to make, there are fundamental themes to be highlighted. Below are a list of questions that the adult can look to when ministering to the adolescent in the area of a moral issue.

Sensitivity:

In what ways is this adolescent sensitive or insensitive?

Can this adolescent view his or her life with a sense of giftedness or gratefulness for who he or she is?

How aware is this adolescent of moral issues when he or she is in various situations? In other words, does the adolescent's level of sensitivity depend on the situation?

Does his or her awareness and sensitivity reflect his or her values?

Does this adolescent's overidentification with a problem prevent him or her from being aware of what is happening?

How needy is this adolescent? (This is often a critical question to ponder when dealing with relationship issues, particularly in the area of sexuality. Feelings such as loneliness, as noted previously, often eclipse a conscious awareness and reflection on moral issues.)

FIGURE 4

ADOLESCENT MORAL DECISION MAKING

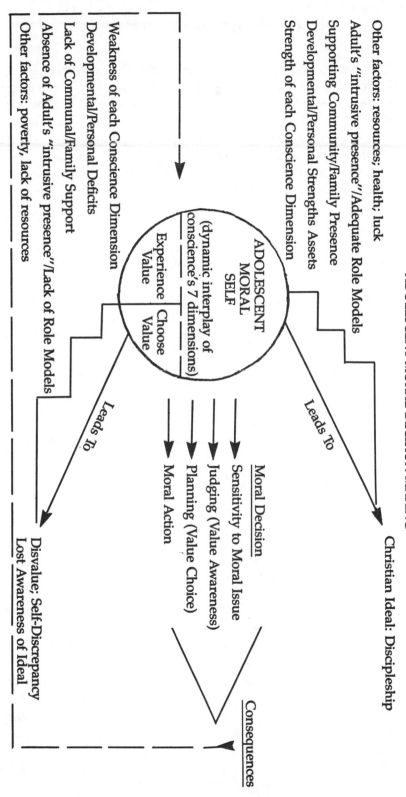

Dimensions of conscience are operative in the adolescent's sensitivity to moral issues. Empathy, above all, is a catalyst for recognizing the moral dimension of an issue. Psychic investment in adaptive and productive tasks fosters maturity and discernment. Avoidance of rationalizing tendencies, for example, encourages healthy defensive functioning, which sustains awareness of a situation and prevents distortion. Idealizations help to form an overall framework for viewing reality, and idealizations that reinforce care and sensitivity encourage recognition of moral issues.

Judgment

How clearly can the adolescent address issues of value?

Does he or she realize the core value issues in this situation?

How does the adolescent deal with conflicts between various values?

What are the criteria the adolescent uses to discern the values present in a situation?

What is the content of the adolescent's moral thinking?

What sources does the adolescent use for forming this content?

How do his or her values reflect who he or she is becoming or desires to be?

Is there a sense of "service" in this adolescent's articulation of value?

Can this adolescent relate his or her values to a personal relationship to Jesus?

How might the adolescent's awareness of value reflect being "true to oneself"—who one is and who one is becoming?

How central to this adolescent are his or her value expressions? In other words, does he or she realize how personal values are a defining expression of who he or she is becoming?

In the judgment component there is a strong teleological dimension. That is, the adolescent searches for reasons for his or her moral recognition. There is deliberation as to the actual value dimensions of the situation and the capacity for self-critique. If the adolescent has been the source for another's hurt or feels that he or she could do something for another, guilt will serve as a focus for examining values. Also, healthy defensive functioning will allow the adolescent to examine a wide variety of values that might be relevant.

150

Planning

What reasons does the adolescent give for his or her choice?

Does this choice create a sense of consistency for the adolescent with other choices he or she has made?

Does this choice show the adolescent as flexible? committed? prudent? realistic? mature? healthy?

Is guilt a factor in this adolescent's choice?

Are there present in this choice some basic unhealthy emotions which are limiting the choice or the decision that is to be made?

The making of moral choices is no doubt complex. It is the very nature of conscience to be the central, dynamic force of such choosing. Above all, idealization—what I am and what I desire to be— becomes a grounding for our choice. Our telic nature, likewise, leads us to understand "why" this choice is made.

Executing

What is encouraging this adolescent to act?

How does the environment support or inhibit the adolescent's choice?

What makes it possible for this adolescent to follow through with this decision?

Most likely, self-esteem is vital for this component. I feel a sense of confidence and ability to initiate an action and respond in a moral fashion. Further, the motivational component of empathic distress provides impetus for my actual response.

It needs to be emphasized that there exists no clear blueprint that tells us exactly "how" these seven dimensions operate among themselves. For that matter, there exists no psychological means to explain the dynamic of conscience as we have sought to describe it. I have simply tried to highlight the influence of some dimensions. I do believe, though, that love and justice necessitate the development of each of these dimensions.

The Decision for Social Justice

The decision for making choices regarding social justice (what we will herein term "social morality") deserves special emphasis. Decisions involving social morality are more conceptually complicated than personal moral decisions (doing something on one's own) or decisions that might be termed interpersonal decisions (involving one's relationship with another). This difficulty arises because social morality includes a distinctive type of awareness and conceptualization. A social justice consciousness involves the understanding and application of moral principles in the context of complex social reality.

Take, for example, the case of Bob, a seventeen-year-old junior high school student. He has recently finished reading a book (for a social studies course) on the history of race relations in the United States. Bob comes from a white middle-class background. He has had little contact with minorities. The stark details in the book about the brutalities of America's social history trouble him. Although he finds it difficult to articulate his feelings, Bob experiences discomfort as he thinks in general about America's treatment of minorities, and, in particular about the extent of discrimination that exists within his own city. Bob's feelings are confirmed by newspaper accounts of recent discrimination and racial problems in various neighborhoods throughout the city.

One should note here that Bob has been able to make an inference from a general moral principle (justice) to a specific application; although often taken for granted, this mental capacity demands a certain level of cognitive sophistication. Bob's empathic concern suggests a central experience required for the development of social morality, empathic distress over the suffering of others. At this point we can view Bob as capable of empathizing not only with individuals but with social groups.

The question does arise as to "why" Bob feels this empathic distress whereas many of his peers might not. One likely answer is that Bob possesses a higher level of empathy. One could speculate that previous learning experiences, most likely in the home, have encouraged his empathic expression. Further, Bob's cognitive functioning has not taken on an egocentric quality that might prevent him for focusing on social problems. In other words, he is aware of his world and his environment.

In addition, it is likely that Bob also evidences a life history that enables him to empathize with others. This includes the sustained experience of peer interactions and friendship experiences. A vital component of experiencing friendship is the mutuality and reciprocal function of rights and duties that children learn. We might even hypothesize that the mutuality and reciprocity learned from childhood and early adolescent friendships form the basis for perceiving the rights and duties of others. Friendships and meaningful peer interactions promote mutuality and more mature understandings of equality and rights—all essential for sustained and enduring friendship. In fact, the interaction among adolescents in peer relationships might well be a crucial determinant in the adolescent's development of social conscience. Unless the adolescent can understand and experience the reciprocal rights and responsibilities inherent in personal relationships and the caring and empathic concerns requisite for personal friendship, a focus on broader groups and people might not be possible. The seeds for a social morality exist in the fertile soil established by nurturing personal relationships.

In a similar vein, the disappointments, inequalities, and hurts sustained in these interpersonal contexts form a psychological foundation for interpreting and making meaningful the hurts and pain experienced by others. Experiencing personal hurt is likely to foster an empathic bonding with those who are less fortunate and who are suffering: "people frequently respond more empathically to others when they themselves have had similar experiences."[14] Even though Bob has not been a victim of racial discrimination, he most likely has experienced other forms of disappointment, perhaps some that are discriminatory. He might have personal characteristics which have made the accomplishments of his own goals doubtful (for example, being too short for the basketball team or being perceived as having too little talent for the school play). Even disappointment in personal relationships (experiences of betrayal, broken confidences) might provide the required psychological experiences for empathizing with individuals and groups who have suffered.

At the same time, the adolescent's experience of personal disappointment and hurt must not be burdensome. If this is the case, then the emotional vicissitudes of adolescence and personal disappointments inherent in any friendship could well foster defensive reactions and too much preoccupation with intrapsychic and interpersonal needs. In sum, there exists the need for what might be termed a *psychological vulnerability* in the adolescent. On the one hand the adolescent must have experienced personal disappointment and hurt, most likely some of which is felt to be unjust. On the other hand, this hurt must not be of such immensity that it induces a level of defensive reactions that inhibit the ability of the adolescent to perceive distress in others while focusing inordinately on the self.

In addition to Bob's sensitivity, he has a need for good judgment. Bob is distressed by what he reads. Yet, his sensitivity must yield to the judgment component—"something must be done." Any analysis of Bob's reaction thus far would lead to the conclusion that some internal standard of his own values have been violated. From the Christian perspective we would interpret this as the functioning of his conscience and Bob's struggle to articulate other-centered value and make it interpretable in the context of social reality.

We have noted that the underlying psychic mechanism that gives impetus to this value formation is the ego ideal. Bob's gradual development of a personal value system includes both the incorporation of parental values and the owning of personal values through the development of a personal ethical code that will guide his own actions through his adult years. The ego ideal fuels this forming of values and the development of a personal value system.

Even so, Bob's increasingly personalized value system is most likely more readily disposed to judgments in terms of personal and interpersonal moral concerns (Should I lie? Should I steal?) than to questions of social morality that include the necessity to evaluate social phenomena as well as political and social issues. Evidence suggests that questions of social and economic inequality (areas in which much social justice education is discussed and presented to adolescents) are perceived much less clearly by children and adolescents than questions of political freedoms, such as issues of free speech.

> Although civil and political rights are clearly perceived as essential in a just society, situations where social or economic justice is involved or where rights come into conflict are considerably more problematic for young people.[15]

Further, evidence seems to indicate that solutions to political and social problems are arrived at with more difficulty than the ability to recognize a problem. "There is little evidence that understanding of remedies for inequality or injustice progresses in a parallel fashion to (or as rapidly as) awareness of injustice or inequality."[16] In sum, Bob must not only be sensitive to injustice, he must also have the reflective capacity to understand the problems that exist as well as some sense that these problems violate or clash with his own values.

Given Bob's sensitivity and his judgment that racial discrimination is wrong, he must now choose to respond in some way. In short, Bob must decide what he will do. At this point, Bob's behavioral choices must confront the complexity of the social reality he wishes to understand. Is the injustice that Bob seeks to respond to the result of complex social conditions? He might, for example, have various interpretations of the reasons for racial discrimination which are conflictual and lead him to make a tentative response. He might be overwhelmed by the amount or the complexity of the social problem or feel he does not have enough information with which to form a judgment.

As Bob formulates his own views on social morality and chooses a course of action, there emerges the potential for conflict with his parents' ideas and beliefs. Bob might favor wholeheartedly the consequences of actions consonant with a social morality in order to distance himself from parental values and beliefs. Thus, Bob might opt for some choices not so much because he believes them, but because they psychically establish his identity and ease separation struggles with parents who perhaps think differently on such issues. On the other hand, some adolescents might resist choosing behaviors consonant with a social morality in order to erase their own fears of separation from parents. Other adolescents might believe they lack the ability to respond to issues important to social morality. Still other adolescents might be disinclined to adopt a social morality perspective simply because of psychological reactance: this is the refusal to choose something because one is told. Thus, if a teacher is seriously invested in social morality, some students might simply prefer to respond negatively in order to be different (or to be for it in order to be different from parents who might be opposed). Finally, some adolescents might have legitimate philosophical differences with some positions of social justice education (e.g., ways to resolve foreign policy conflicts, amount to spend on military defense), and their views need to be given respect and consideration.

Ideally, the most developed understanding of social morality includes not only behaviors which respond to the pain and oppression of others, but which also mirror an increasingly sophisticated level of value formation. At the same time, in the midst of this increasing sophistication, one's set of beliefs must not be rigidly held but flexible in order to accommodate new experiences and challenges to currently held beliefs and values.

Having made a choice, Bob must now act on his choice. His action could take many forms. Bob could write a letter to the newspaper, join a club which engages in social action, give money to a charity, take part in a demonstration. Other forms of expression might be a conscious effort to seek out minority students or to read more deeply in various areas of social justice. The ability for Bob to respond in a positive fashion toward issues of social morality is in large part a function of Bob's own self-esteem and maturity level. This maturity includes the ability to fulfill one's goals and carry out one's desires. Also, a sense of self-efficacy regarding his behaviors is noted. Psychologist Ervin Staub has noted "belief in one's ability to influence events and bring about desired outcomes seems important in leading people to initiate action and actively pursue goals, except when the required action is easy and straightforward."[17] Obviously, issues of social justice, which are often complex, require a necessary level of self-esteem in order for positive and constructive behaviors to be initiated.

The Adolescent's Everyday Decision and the "Pastoral Moment"

An adolescent informed me recently of a personal decision he was attempting to resolve. He wanted to leave his part-time work and find a related line of work that offered more creativity and freedom (but less pay). Around the same time I had a conversation with a former student who was wondering which of several college majors she might pursue. She was attracted to both social work and management science and wondered which would bring her more satisfaction.

The underlying theme of these situations is the necessity for everyday choosing. It is this everyday deciding—the need to "transform" (Rom. 12:2) our everyday choices and decisions—that at times renders life both perplexing and frustrating. No doubt we all have, or will eventually confront, serious moral challenges. Deciding the fate of a family member on life-support systems, attempting to cope with the possibility of an impending divorce, confronting a serious crisis of faith, or accepting a decision calling for retribution or commitment to a deeper level of justice are just a few of the major ethical dilemmas that might invade our lives and call forth a deeper level of Christian self-awareness and commitment.

But so often it is not these major moral dilemmas but everyday decisions that preoccupy our time and effort. It is the concrete realities of the everyday—a business move, a response we make in a personal relationship, acceptance of volunteer work, a decision to purchase or not purchase a particular good—that give our Christian lives their real test. It would be much easier if our choice were between clearly perceived good or evil, yet we know that everyday decisions are rarely that simple! Far more likely we are faced with various options, all of which are attractive, and we find ourselves sorting through the choices attempting to discover what might be the "best" Christian response. Which way should I go? What choice is best? How can I decide this matter? This everyday choosing enables us to express the meaning of our Christian lives. More than anything, everyday Christian decision making needs points of reference that help to clarify our Christian commitment and translate our moral stances into everyday choices.

Two significant events in theology have helped shed light on everyday Christian decision making. First, recent development in spirituality highlight for Christians the importance of priority to the question, Where is God leading me now? Popular interest in discernment—the conscious attention to the Lord's movements within one's own life—provides a vital focus for awareness of the Lord's beckoning. Second, moral theology's recent stress on the person as a moral agent and on the need for personal acceptance and responsibility for "my" moral decisions lends support to a decision-making process that is personal, responsible, and maturing.

Ideally, then, everyday Christian decision making takes account of our own conscious realization of the Lord's presence in our lives and elicits in each of us a deepening awareness and care for our brothers and sisters (other-centered value) as we encounter everyday decisions and choices.

The adolescent encounters a number of decisions in his or her life that require distinct moral choices between good and evil. Often these struggles are made difficult because of peer pressure, or the lack of a mature identity. The adolescent who rejects using drugs or practices self-control or refuses to go along with the peer group's stereotypic responses toward others is attempting to search for a good rooted in Gospel value. In such an adolescent there emerges the articulation and personal appropriation of other-centered value. A general guideline when attempting to interpret adolescent choices is the following: The less coherent the sense of personal identity, the more the adolescent is apt to rely on external sources of support for moral guidance, whether it be the dictates of parents or the pressure of the peer group, or the allurements of the culture.

Yet, like adults, adolescents are often confronted in their everyday lives by innumerable choices that, for the most part, are not questions of good versus evil. Everyday choices can be envisioned as multiple paths that adolescents might choose (all of which are legitimate) as they move toward adulthood. In other words, the constant everyday choosing the adolescent experiences becomes, with time, the building blocks of a growing sense of adulthood. This growth often appears subtle, yet the gradual making of choices becomes the foundation for further choosing and increasingly defines both a style of choosing and the reasons for choice.

Everyday choices in adolescence deserve attention. Growth in the moral life is not reflected in dramatic leaps. On the contrary, growing more deeply in the moral self is more accurately portrayed as a gradual, evolving process that provides, in its ideal context, deepening levels of self-insight as well as corresponding freedom. Accepting the consequences of previously made choices, no matter how commonplace or mundane, helps to mold a deepening sense of one's moral self. As years go by, a deepening reflective capacity and growing maturity allow the adolescent to view life choices through a template of values. However, this template, which reflects a deepening commitment to the Lord and Gospel values, must be consistently pointed out to the adolescent. The adult, by his role and presence in the adolescent's life, can encourage this growing moral sensitivity.

I have found that the best way for the adult to aid the adolescent's growth in moral sensitivity is by being what I term an "articulator of value." Sometimes this distinct presence is best displayed to the adolescent by mere silence, which affords the adolescent the opportunity, the time and place, for quiet reflection. At other times, a more direct approach is indicated. Posing specific questions not only addresses the need to articulate value, it also focuses the adolescent's attention on the significance of the choice and what the choice reflects about the adolescent's own sense of core value.

Making significant moral decisions is integral to the growth of the adolescent's moral self. In addition, though, there is the vast area of adolescent everyday choosing. The opportunity to reflect with the adolescent on everyday decisions is what I term the "pastoral moment." This term implies an attempt on the adult's part to provide the adolescent with the opportunity for clarity and deeper reflection. Everyday decisions are not subject to drawn-out counseling sessions. Rather, they often take only a few minutes discussion when the adult provides a thought or reflection for the adolescent to ponder. The adolescent need not respond at that moment. I often simply ask the adolescent just to "think about that" at some future point before a choice is made. The pastoral moment involves presenting to the adolescent some criteria, often just one or two, that will expand his or her consciousness and enable a richer and fuller response of value to be made.

Below are some specific criteria that are helpful to share with the adolescent as the learning aspect of the "pastoral moment." As noted above, I have found it best simply to share one or two of these at any one sitting (moment) with the adolescent.

1. Jesus

For Christians the focus in life is always on the life, death, and resurrection of Jesus. In the context of this faith commitment we respond to Jesus' call to "come follow me" (Mark 10:21). Saint Ignatius perceptively noted this invitation of Jesus when posing the questions, "What have I done for Christ?" "What do I do for Christ?" and "What will I do for Christ?" When making everyday decisions, an important question is the presence of Jesus in this choice. If, for example, an adolescent is wondering whether to take on volunteer work or some other activity, there is a need to consider how this choice allows the adolescent to experience the presence of Christ in his or her life. What would Jesus say about this work in light of my present life situation (other obligations, time involvement, personal talents, and so on)? Every Christian needs to reflect on his or her personal experience of Jesus, and how this choice allows Jesus to become a greater mediating influence in his or her life. I have often simply asked an adolescent the question, "Have you asked Jesus to help you with the decision?" or "How much has Jesus been a part of your choice?" I caution the adolescent that, of course, the Lord will not give a crystal-clear answer and direct the decision. I do say that friends, though, like to know our choices and concerns, and if the Lord is a friend then it stands to reason that we share with him our concerns.

2. Community

Christian living is never done in a vacuum. Our decisions and choices are inextricably tied to the roles and relationships that envelop our lives. If we choose to leave a certain occupation, we touch not only our own life but the lives of family, friends, and associates. Our decision, in other words, is not unrelated to other relationships in our life. When choosing a line of work or a college major, we are asked to consider the needs and life situations of others, too. Our decisions, likewise, are made real in the life of a community that has a unique heritage and tradition. As we have already noted, Saint Paul was adamant in his dealings with the people of Corinth about the eating of certain foods and speaking in tongues. Christians, says Saint Paul, need awareness of their brothers and sisters, always being attentive to their needs. For Paul, if eating certain foods causes scandal, or if emphasis on speaking in tongues overshadows others' gifts within the community, then these behaviors must be altered out of respect for other members. As Christians we must ask where the community of faith fits into our decisions and choices. How does the decision that we make reconcile us with the needs and desires of others within the community of faith whose tradition we embrace? If we keep up with current events, for example, and we choose to take part in political activities, we need to seek knowledge of our own faith community's stance on questions of politics and related social concerns. If we choose to dissent from our community's stance, we need to say why this is so and be willing both to offer input to the faith community and at the same time to be aware of the reasons why the faith community's stance differs from our own. Often, due to their own egocentric style, adolescents are oblivious of the impact their decisions have on others. I often find it useful simply to ask the adolescent "In what ways will your decision influence or impact on others?" "Have you thought of this fact?" "Is there some way that this realization might affect your decision?"

3. Love

The great Christian commandment is love (John 15:12) and Christians are called to a loving relationship of universal openness toward others. The love that Paul so eloquently describes as patient, kind, not rude, not boastful, bearing all things, believing all things, hoping all things, enduring all things (1 Cor. 13:4–7) is a distinguishing mark for Christians. Thus, if we are making a decision in regard to the use of our time, we might well refer to Paul and ask how we are becoming more loving through care, kindness, and genuine human attentiveness as a result of this decision. If we take on some hobby, we would do well to ask ourselves how, with this new commitment, our Christian love is made real for those with whom we work, live, and play. In effect, is this choice the more loving thing to do at this moment in my life? Regarding adolescents, I have found that the simplest way to express this is to ask the adolescent simply, "How are you more loving if you do this?" "Have you ever thought of that?" "What choice would make you more loving?"

4. Solitude

When making a choice, we should be concerned not only with content (what particular thing I should do), but also with the process of actual decision making (the steps I use in making this decision). All too often our focus is restricted to the area of content. Yet, an essential component of Christian decision making is attention to how this decision is made, and an integral factor in the Christian process is solitude. "Rising early the next morning, he went off to a lonely place in the desert; there he was absorbed in prayer" (Mark 1:35). What strikes us in reading Scripture is Jesus' fidelity to his own life of solitude. In our own lives, too, we must look for moments of aloneness. If a job, an activity, or a purchase are so important, might not their real meaningfulness become more understandable through reflecting on these choices? I usually encourage adolescents to find a quiet place or some type of solitude that will enable them to sort out and reflect upon their choices.

5. Openness

Allied with the above need for solitude is the need for openness. Are we willing to seek the advice of others, to ask others for their opinions and counsel? Trusted friends and experienced professionals can provide a conduit for valuable insights while offering a richer perspective for our choices. Saint Ignatius suggests that inclinations to keep to ourselves can reflect serious temptations, since we beguile ourselves and cut off the very human openness that brings clarity to our Christian lives. He labels this temptation to silence as arising from a "false lover" whose manipulations entrap us. When facing a particular choice, we need an openness and sharing that sheds light on our interior disposition. Thus, if we wonder whether a relationship is truly growthful, we should seek counsel from friends we trust. Failure to seek enlightening dialogue with others renders us susceptible to the numerous personal limits and misconceptions that detach us from our own moral growth. In this light, I always thank any adolescent who shares some choice or decision that he or she must make. I also ask the adolescent to identify other people he or she might trust or wish to seek counsel from.

6. Growth

The Christian obligation is not only to be in Christ (Gal. 3:20) but through this union with Christ to "increase and abound" in love for others (1Thess. 3:12). Saint Paul characterizes his own growth in the Lord as a "race" in which the "prize" is "life on high in Christ Jesus" (Phil. 3:12–14). Two focuses are particularly helpful here. First, how have previous choices in our life contributed to our being who we are today? Similarly, we must ask how we have grown in love through these past decisions, especially as they relate to the present choice we are making. One might reflect, likewise, on what previous choices most touch our present decision. If, for example, we are facing an occupational choice, we would do well to ask what past decisions have brought us to this present moment (college major, vocational interest, some activity that fosters personal talents). How have previous choices contributed to who we are, and how have these decisions allowed us to give ourselves increasingly in a spirit of Christian selflessness to others? Second, we might project ourselves several years into the future and look at what we perceive to be the consequences of this present decision, particularly as it pertains to our own moral growth. How do we foresee this choice as leading us to greater Christian growth in both the love and care we show ourselves and others? We might also imaginatively rehearse in our minds the future possibilities before us. As we reflect on the alternatives that we foresee, we would do well to gauge our own affective responses as well as ask the question, "How am I growing as a Christian through this choice?"

7. Limitations

Regardless of the choices we make, no matter how well intentioned we are, our own lives demonstrate our inadequacies and limits. Every Christian can empathize with Paul's own struggles to follow the Spirit's call. "I cannot even understand my own actions; I do not do what I want to do but what I hate" (Rom. 7:15). In addition to our personal limits, we find ourselves challenged by the confines of our culture (stereotypes, narrow attitudes) and the painful realities of our own life situation (lack of skills, time, financial resources). Conclusively, though, our choices never succeed in completely appropriating the Gospel's command to love. This knowledge of limits calls us to reflect more deeply on our choices. Just as we must look at the opportunities that allow us to love, so too must we center on the limiting, narrowing, and unloving aspects of our decisions. What are the unloving possibilities which might result from this choice? Interpreting our life history means recognizing our blindness and nongrowthful ways of behaving that are incompatible with following the Lord. By recognizing and admitting our weaknesses (2 Cor. 12:10), we are led to rely on decisions nourished by Jesus' presence and nurtured through prayer and sacramental participation. I encourage adolescents to think about the limiting nature of their choices and to examine aspects of themselves that might limit their decision. This type of intrusion into the adolescent's life should be entered cautiously and attention paid to the adolescent's level of self-insight and self-esteem. Nonetheless, adolescents can often be challenged to examine their own limitations; often it takes the adult's intrusive presence to foster the necessary insight.

8. Affectivity

Depth psychology has revealed the critical influence that feelings have on our attitudes, perceptions, and behavior. Theologians, likewise, note the central role affective responses have for a maturing faith. Ideally, my actual feelings dispose me to respond more freely in a more authentic faith commitment. No doubt my decisions can flow from numerous unrecognized feelings, such as anger, fear, or jealousy. From another perspective, we cannot dismiss the role that environments have on our behaviors. Our internal psychological states—such as tiredness, stress, low self-esteem, feelings of personal inadequacy—all unite to undermine and circumvent Christian growth. Authentic choosing encourages us to look within ourselves and be aware of these numerous feelings that interweave with our attempts to choose authentic Christian responses. Naturally, it is important that we take time to examine what feelings might be operative in our decision making. I often will simply ask the adolescent what his or her feelings were as this choice was thought through. Sometimes I will encourage the adolescent to find some solitude, to imagine the decision and note the feelings that are present. I then ask the adolescent to reflect on what these feelings might be saying about the decision contemplated.

9. Responsibility

When professing Christian commitment we must be responsible for the decisions we make. As Christians we are called to make choices that reflect our responsible use of Christian freedom (Gal. 5:13–14). Our choosing represents a loving presence in our life as we grow more and more responsible. And in accepting responsibility we also commit ourselves to the prospect of altering or tempering our choices as subsequent experiences enter into our life history. What orients our decisions are not rigid commitments to past choices but the presence of Jesus Christ and his message of incarnating love (Matt. 22:39). This paradoxical dynamic whereby Christian freedom is lived in a growing dependency on Christ leads to deepening personal choices based on a growing Christian maturity (Phil. 3:15). In this regard, I sometimes ask adolescents if they feel themselves becoming more an adult. I then ask them to relate this "feeling" of being an adult to the decisions they make.

CHAPTER FIVE

Morality, the Adolescent, and the Future

Several days ago I took a short break from my writing and wandered through the Jesuit community library. I took a few moments and browsed through the books on religious education and pastoral ministry, paying particular attention to those published several decades ago, in the 1950s and sixties. What struck me was the sense of certainty these books conveyed to the reader. In working with youth, there seemed in these books to be readily available answers—it was all right there.

I am not sure that the reader of this book has such a felt sense of security. Indeed, pastoral ministry to youth in the late 1980s and beyond is anything but certain! At the same time, however, I would hope that the reader of these pages will realize the significance of his or her own actions when working with youth, as well as the excitement and challenge that such work entails. More than anything, these pages have attempted to convey the vital significance of the adult's presence for the adolescent's moral growth. There can be no greater priority for a faith community than the development of the moral consciousness of its young people. Without this thrust as a central mission of its work, the community's very viability as a community of disciples and a prophetic witness is compromised.

I would like to conclude with several points. First, the cultural climate in which we live these waning years of the twentieth century is anything but conducive to the development of moral sensitivity. As Robert Coles notes, "for some young people, much of our culture is a second bad home."[1] The poisoning climate of drug abuse, the tenuous nature of family life, the allures of materialism, and the constant battle for impulse control in the midst of ready sex and the never-ending stream of consumerism makes the role of the adult minister all the more significant in the lives of youth today. Viewed another way, the adult's presence can provide a ready point of reference for the adolescent who is facing all too many obstacles along the road to adulthood.

In addition, in my clinical and pastoral work I have increasingly experienced (and have grown increasingly concerned) about a phenomenon I have noticed in some parents. For lack of a better term I will label it "parental paralysis." All too often, many parents are bewildered by the stresses and strains of parenting, are unsure of the moral values they should be articulating to their children, or if they are clear as to what values they wish to convey, they are unclear as to just how this might be done. This feeling of paralysis has led them to question their own roles as parents and, in some cases, led them to adopt an almost laissez-faire approach to parenting. In such instances, the role of the adult minister is all the more vital in filling the void left by parental uncertainty. To be sure, the vast majority of parents strive to exert a moral presence in their child's life. Yet, the growing sense of self-doubt that I have witnessed is a concern.

In addition to this self-doubt, I believe there exists a "personal" reason why many parents find it difficult to be sharers of moral values with their children. Stated simply, in addition to the stress and insecurity that many adolescents experience, there are a great number of parents who are under a considerable if not overwhelming degree of stress, too. In chapter 3 we spoke of the need for an adequate level of psychic energy to be invested in life tasks. For a variety of reasons that includes the stress of modern life, the pressures of dual-career or one-parent families, financial issues, personal life issues, or the combination of some if not all of these, parents often lack enough energy to provide adequate parenting without extraordinary if not heroic sacrifice.

Finally, and most tragically, there are some homes that are so dysfunctional—homes where the psychological hurt is so deep and parents as adult human beings are so wounded—that parents simply do not have the psychological resources to offer their children adequate role models. In these homes, parents often are inevitably invested in their own selves and do not have the adequate psychological capacities to provide for their children, even though they often desire to be present to them.

For all these reasons, the role of the adult who ministers to youth—whether as teacher, counselor, youth minister, or some other—takes on more and more significance. Moreover, I have no doubt that the role of adult witness in the faith community will grow with respect to an increasing professionalism. In this regard, there will be greater and greater need for the adult to be readily available to youth as a witness to Gospel values. Given this reality, increasingly adult ministers will need to have a wide degree of self-knowledge in order that their relationship with adolescents will be an encounter of openness and trust rather than a perceived or imagined threat or fear. Likewise, there will be the need for the adult minister to be knowledgeable about the faith's community understanding of a wide variety of issues, and be willing to dialogue with the adolescent regarding endless questioning of sexual matters or the ongoing debate of the Christian's role in the modern world, and to carry on such dialogue in an informative as well as receptive way.

To journey with the adolescent on the road to moral maturity is no doubt a trip that will have many twists and turns. Along this journey, the adult's compassionate sensitivity and loving challenge can be a steady guide. More than anything, it is the church's offer of help to her young people that will be the best guarantee for the future that, to a searching and troubled world, "Christ is being proclaimed!" (Phil. 1:18).

Notes

Chapter 1. Defining Adolescent Morality

1. American Psychiatric Association, *A Psychiatric Glossary*, 4th ed. (Washington, D. C.: APA, 1975), p. 48; quoted in Armand M. Nicholi, Jr., "The Adolescent," in *The Harvard Guide to Modern Psychiatry*, ed. Armand M. Nicholi, Jr. (Cambridge: Harvard University Press, 1978), p. 519.

2. Timothy E. O'Connell, "A Theology of Sin," *Chicago Studies* 21 (Fall 1982): 278.

3. Barbel Inhelder and Jean Piaget, *The Growth of Logical Thinking from Childhood to Adolescence* (New York: Basic Books, 1968), p. 343.

4. David Elkind, "Child Development and Counseling," *The Personnel and Guidance Journal* 58 (January 1980): 61.

5. James Fowler and Sam Keen, *Life Maps* (Waco, TX: Word Books, 1978), p. 61.

6. Daniel Goleman, "Teen-Age Risk Taking: Rise in Deaths Prompts New Research Effort," *New York Times*, November 24, 1987, p. 16.

7. For a discussion of this issue, see William M. Kurtines and Jacob L. Gewirtz, "Certainty and Morality: Objectivistic versus Relativistic Approaches," in *Morality, Moral Behavior, and Moral Development*, ed. William M. Kurtines and Jacob L. Gewirtz (New York: John Wiley, 1984), pp. 3–23.

8. A brief and accurate discussion of Kohlberg's work can be found in Ronald Duska and Mariellen Whelan, *Moral Development: A Guide to Piaget and Kohlberg* (New York: Paulist Press, 1975). I believe a weakness of this book is the authors' uncritical acceptance of much of Kohlberg's theory. Though in fairness to the authors, at the time the text was written uncritical acceptance of Kohlberg was "the" popular response.

9. Lawrence Kohlberg, "Education, Moral Development, and Faith," *Journal of Moral Education* 4 (October 1974): 5.

10. The brief outline of Kohlberg's theory described in this chapter is the most well-known view of his theory. It should be pointed out, however, that Kohlberg has renamed his stages after more extensive research. The new terms for his stages are the following: Stage One: Heteronomous Morality; Stage Two: Individualistic, Instrumental Morality; Stage Three: Interpersonally Normative Morality; Stage Four: Social Systems Morality; Stage Five: Human Rights and Social Welfare Morality; Stage Six: Morality of Universalizable, Reversible, and Prescriptive General Ethical Principles. Many have found these revisions to be bewildering. The commonly accepted notion of his theory is the one contained in this chapter. We will use the more traditional formulation and note changes and alterations of his theory when necessary. For a discussion of Kohlberg's more recent research, see Lawrence Kohlberg, *The Psychology of Moral Development* (San Francisco: Harper & Row, 1984).

11. Lawrence Kohlberg and Carol Gilligan, "The Adolescent as a Philosopher: The Discovery of Self in a Postconventional World," *Daedalus* 100 (Fall 1971): 1066–67.

12. Lawrence Kohlberg, "Educating for a Just Society," in *Moral Development, Moral Education, and Kohlberg,* ed. Brenda Munsey (Birmingham, AL: Religious Education Press, 1980), pp. 458–59.

13. Charles M. Shelton, S.J., *Adolescent Spirituality: Pastoral Ministry for High School and College Youth* (Chicago: Loyola University Press, 1983; paperback ed. New York: Crossroad, 1989).

14. Arnold A. Lazarus, *The Practice of Multi-Modal Therapy* (New York: McGraw-Hill, 1981).

15. Fowler and Keen, *Life Maps*, p. 61.

16. Kohlberg and Gilligan, "The Adolescent as Philosopher," p. 1074.

17. For a discussion of the relationship between empathy and ministry, see Charles M. Shelton, S.J., "Christian Empathy: The Psychological Foundation for Pastoral Ministry," *Chicago Studies* 23 (August 1984): 209–22.

18. Gerald Grant, "The Character of Education and the Education of Character," *Daedalus* 110 (Summer 1981): 144.

19. Jerome Kagan, "The Moral Function of the School," *Daedalus* 110 (Summer 1981): 162.

20. Ibid., p. 163.

Chapter 2. A Psychological Model for Adolescent Morality

1. See James R. Rest, "Morality," in *Handbook of Child Psychology*, vol. 3, *Cognitive Development*, ed. Paul H. Mussen (New York: John Wiley, 1983),

pp. 556–629; James L. Carroll and James R. Rest, "Moral Development," in *Handbook of Developmental Psychology,* ed. Benjamin J. Wolman (Englewood Cliffs, NJ: Prentice-Hall, 1982), pp. 434–51; James R. Rest, "The Major Components of Morality," in *Morality, Moral Behavior, and Moral Development,* ed. William M. Kurtines and Jacob L. Gewirtz (New York: John Wiley, 1984), pp. 24–40; James R. Rest, "An Interdisciplinary Approach to Moral Education," in *Moral Education: Theory and Application,* ed. Marvin W. Berkowitz and Fritz Oser (Hillsdale, NJ: Lawrence Erlbaum, 1985), pp. 9–26.

2. Rest, "Morality," p. 558.

3. Rest, "An Interdisciplinary Approach to Moral Education," p. 14.

4. These four components are described extensively in the four articles cited above. The reader is encouraged to read Rest's articles for a fuller explanation of his views.

5. John H. Wright, S.J., "The Hermeneutics of Eschatology," *Chicago Studies* 24 (October 1985): 219.

6. Mihaly Csikszentmihalyi and Reed Larson, *Being Adolescent* (New York: Basic Books, 1984), p. 235.

7. Peter Blos, *On Adolescence* (New York: 1962), p. 184.

8. For a discussion of this issue, see Joseph Sandler, Alex Holder, and Dale Meers, "The Ego Ideal and the Ideal Self," in *The Psychoanalytic Study of the Child,* vol. 18, ed. Ruth Eissler, Anna Freud, Heinz Hartmann, and Marianne Kris (New York: International Universities Press, 1963), pp. 139–58.

9. Peter Blos, "The Function of the Ego Ideal in Adolescence," in *The Psychoanalytic Study of the Child,* vol. 27, ed. Ruth Eissler, Anna Freud, Marianne Kris, and Albert Solnit (New York: Quadrangle Books, 1973), p. 95.

Chapter 3. Conscience and the Adolescent Moral Self

1. See, for example, Robert N. Emde, William F. Johnson, and M. Ann Easterbrooks, "The Do's and Don'ts of Early Moral Development: Psychoanalytic Tradition and Current Research," in *The Emergence of Morality in Young Children,* ed. Jerome Kagan and Sharon Lamb (Chicago: University of Chicago Press, 1987), pp. 245–76; Martin L. Hoffman, "Developmental Synthesis of Affect and Cognition and Its Implications for Altruistic Motivation," *Developmental Psychology* 11 (September 1975): 607–22; Martin L. Hoffman, "Is Altruism Part of Human Nature?" *Journal of Personality and Social Psychology* 40 (January 1981): 121–37.

2. See Timothy E. O'Connell, *Principles for a Catholic Morality* (New York: Seabury Press, 1978).

3. For an overview of conscience from the Catholic Christian perspective see Rudolf Hoffman, "Conscience," in *Encyclopedia of Theology: The Concise Sacramentum Mundi*, ed. Karl Rahner, S.J. (New York: Seabury Press, 1975), pp.283–88. I am indebted to this article for scripture quotes concerning conscience.

4. Robert J. Campbell, "Superego and Conscience," in *Conscience, Its Freedom and Limitations*, ed. William C. Bier, S.J. (New York: Fordham University Press, 1971), p. 83.

5. Barbara M. Stillwell and Matthew Galvin, "Conceptualization of Conscience in 11–12-Year-Olds," *Journal of the American Academy of Child Psychiatry* 24 (1985): 630–36.

6. For an excellent discussion of this issue see Eli Sagan, *Freud, Women, and Morality* (New York: Basic Books, 1988).

7. See ibid. and Robert N. Emde et al., "The Do's and Don'ts of Early Moral Development."

8. Emde et al.,"The Do's and Don'ts of Early Moral Development."

9. Eli Sagan, *Freud, Women, and Morality*, p. 9.

10. Ibid., p. 18.

11. David Shapiro, *Neurotic Styles* (New York: Basic Books, 1965), pp. 163–64.

12. Mihaly Csikszentmihalyi and Reed Larson, *Being Adolescent* (New York: Basic Books, 1984), p. 12. I would endorse their view that psychic energy can be viewed as attention.

13. Ibid., p. 14.

14. For an excellent discussion of defense mechanisms, see William W. Meissner, S.J., "Theories of Personality and Psychopathology: Classical Psychoanalysis," in *Comprehensive Textbook of Psychiatry*, vol. 4, ed. Harold I. Kaplan and Benjamin J. Sadock (New York: William & Wilkins, 1985), pp. 388–90.

15. Robert Coles and Geoffrey Stokes, *Sex and the American Teenager* (New York: Harper & Row/Rolling Stone Press), p. 200.

16. For the etiology of compulsive care-giving, see John Bowlby, "Attachment Theory and Its Therapeutic Implications," in *Adolescent Psychiatry*, vol. 6, ed. Sherman C. Feinstein and Peter L. Giovacchini (Chicago: University of Chicago Press, 1978), pp. 5–33.

17. William W. Meissner, S.J., "Theories of Personality and Psychopathology," p. 390.

18. Martin Hoffman has written extensively in this area. For an understanding of his theory, the following are recommended: Martin L. Hoffman, "Moral Development in Adolescence," in *Handbook of Adolescent Psychology*, ed. Joseph Adelson (New York: John Wiley, 1980), pp. 295–343; Martin L. Hoffman, "Development of Prosocial Motivation: Empathy and

Guilt," in *The Development of Prosocial Behavior*, ed. Nancy Eisenberg (New York: Academic Press, 1982), pp. 281–313. I rely on these texts for this short summary of his empathic theory. I view Hoffman's ideas as having profound significance for pastoral education. I plan to detail the significance of his thinking in later writing.

19. See reference above for a more detailed examination of Hoffman's ideas regarding guilt.

20. Martin L. Hoffman, "Development of Prosocial Motivation: Empathy and Guilt," p. 299.

21. See Charles M. Shelton, S.J., "The Adolescent, Social Justice, and the Catholic School," *The Living Light* 17 (Fall 1980): 223–33.

22. Janine Chassequet-Smirgel, *The Ego Ideal: A Psychoanalytic Essay on the Malady of the Ideal* (New York: W. W. Norton, 1985), p. 29.

23. Ibid., p. 30.

24. Jerome Kagan, *The Nature of the Child* (New York: Basic Books, 1984), p. 145.

25. Joseph F. Rychlak, *Discovering Free Will and Personal Responsibility* (New York: Oxford University Press, 1979), p. 148. I would recommend this book for a discussion of free will and personal responsibility from a psychological perspective.

26. Ibid.

27. Robert Atkinson, "The Development of Purpose in Adolescence: Insights from the Narrative Approach," in *Adolescent Psychiatry*, vol. 14, ed. Sherman C. Feinstein (Chicago: University of Chicago Press), pp. 160–61.

28. I am indebted to the article by James Gaffney and his stimulating discussion for the idea of using the David story. See James Gaffney, "Moral Views and Moral Viewpoints," *America* 158 (January 23, 1988), pp. 55–8, 76.

29. Ibid., p. 56.

30. Ibid.

31. Pierre Ganne, S.J., "Who Do You Say That I Am?" *Cross Currents* 33 (Spring 1983): 18.

32. James R. Rest, "The Major Components of Morality," in *Morality, Moral Behavior, and Moral Development*, ed. William M. Kurtines and Jacob L. Gewirtz (New York: John Wiley, 1984), p. 32.

33. Augusto Blasi, "Moral Identity: Its Role in Moral Functioning," in *Morality, Moral Behavior, and Moral Development*, ed. Kurtines and Gewirtz (New York: John Wiley, 1984), p. 131.

34. Erik Erikson, "The Concept of Ego Identity," *Journal of the American Psychoanalytic Association* 4 (1956): 179.

35. Erik Erikson, "Reflections on Dr. Borg's Life Cycle," in *Adulthood*, ed. Erik Erikson (New York: W. W. Norton, 1978), p. 28.

36. William Damon, "Self-Understanding and Moral Development from Childhood to Adolescence," in *Morality, Moral Behavior, and Moral Development*, ed. Kurtines and Gewirtz (New York: John Wiley, 1984), p. 112.

37. Ibid., p. 116.

38. Ibid., p. 119.

39. Ibid.

40. Ibid.

41. James Youniss, *Parents and Peers in Social Development* (Chicago: University of Chicago Press, 1980).

42. Robert Kegan, *The Evolving Self* (Cambridge, MA: Harvard University Press, 1982).

43. William Damon, "Self-Understanding and Moral Development from Childhood to Adolescence," p. 116.

Chapter 4. Helping Adolescents Make Moral Decisions

1. Stephen Brion-Meisels and Robert L. Selman, "The Adolescent as Interpersonal Negotiator: Three Portraits of Social Development," *Moral Education: Theory and Application*, ed. Marvin W. Berkowitz and Fritz Oser (Hillsdale, NJ: Lawrence Erlbaum, 1985), p. 370.

2. Mihaly Csikszentmihalyi and Reed Larson, *Being Adolescent* (New York: Basic Books, 1984), pp. 235–36.

3. Ibid., pp. 19–23.

4. Ibid., p. 180.

5. Eric Ostrov and Daniel Offer, "Loneliness and the Adolescent," in *Adolescent Psychiatry*, vol. 6, ed. Sherman C. Feinstein and Peter L. Giovacchini (Chicago: University of Chicago Press, 1978), p. 36.

6. Csikszentmihalyi and Larson, *Being Adolescent*, p. 282.

7. Ibid., p. 278.

8. Anthony de Mello, S.J., *Wellsprings* (Garden City, NY: Image Books, 1986), p. 227.

9. David L. Fleming, S.J., *The Spiritual Exercises: A Literal Translation and a Contemporary Reading* (St. Louis: Institute of Jesuit Sources, 1978), p. 13.

10. Philip S. Keane, S.S., *Christian Ethics and Imagination* (New York: Paulist Press, 1984), p. 81.

11. Ibid., p. 82.

12. John English, S.J., *Choosing Life*, (New York: Paulist Press, 1978), p. 10.

13. Ibid., p. 11.

14. Ervin Staub, *Positive Social Behavior and Morality: Social and Personal Influences* (New York: Academic Press, 1978), p. 138.

15. Judith Torney-Purta, "The Development of Views About the Role of Social Institutions in Redressing Inequality and Promoting Human Rights," in *The Child's Construction of Social Inequality,* ed. Robert L. Leahy (New York: Academic Press, 1983), p. 300.

16. Ibid., p. 308.

17. Ervin Staub, *Positive Social Behavior and Morality,* p. 55.

Chapter 5. Morality, the Adolescent, and the Future

1. Robert Coles, "Adolescence Listening to the Youth of the '80s," *Sojourners* 17 (April 1988), p. 18. The quote by Coles contained in the Introduction is also from this article, p. 19.

Index